10/07

D0148976

Insult to Injury

Insult to Injury

Rethinking Our Responses to Intimate Abuse

LINDA G. MILLS

PRINCETON UNIVERSITY PRESS
PRINCETON AND OXFORD

Published by Princeton University Press, 41 William Street, Princeton,
New Jersey 08540

In the United Kingdom: Princeton University Press, 3 Market Place, Woodstock,
Oxfordshire OX20 1SY

Library of Congress Cataloging-in-Publication Data
Mills, Linda G.
  Insult to injury : rethinking our responses to intimate abuse / Linda G. Mills.
    p. cm.
  Includes bibliographical references and index.
ISBN 0-691-09639-2 (cloth : alk. paper)
1. Family violence. 2. Conjugal violence. 3. Wife abuse. 4. Abusive men.
5. Abusive women. 6. Feminist theory. I. Title.
HV66260.M55 2003
362.82′92—dc21   2003044476

British Library Cataloging-in-Publication Data is available

This book has been composed in Goudy

Printed on acid-free paper. ∞

www.pupress.princeton.edu

Printed in the United States of America

10 9 8 7 6 5 4 3 2 1

For Peter

    — who taught me there was so much more to love

And for Ronnie

    — who insists we learn these lessons

— Try to Praise the Mutilated World

Try to praise the mutilated world.
Remember June's long days,
and wild strawberries, drops of wine, the dew.
The nettles that methodically overgrow
the abandoned homesteads of exiles.
You must praise the mutilated world.
You watched the stylish yachts and ships;
one of them had a long trip ahead of it,
while salty oblivion awaited others.
You've seen the refugees going nowhere,
you've heard the executioners sing joyfully.
You should praise the mutilated world.
Remember the moments when we were together
in a white room and the curtain fluttered.
Return in thought to the concert where music flared.
You gathered acorns in the park in autumn
and leaves eddied over the earth's scars.
Praise the mutilated world
and the gray feather a thrush lost,
and the gentle light that strays and vanishes
and returns.

—Adam Zagajewski

Contents

~ Giving Thanks

THESE FEW PAGES CANNOT DO JUSTICE TO THE PEOPLE who helped me formulate these ideas and commit them to paper. I owe an incalculable debt to Heather Abel, who questioned nearly every line for the purpose of clarifying and improving my argument. She did so with a genius only I can truly appreciate and with a generosity that can come only from the truly gifted. Heather's insight, passion, and enthusiasm maintained mine when my own commitment to the project waned. Marisa Howe, a law student at New York University, worked meticulously on checking citations and grammar, always with a sense of humor about the absurdity of my demands. She made the process bearable and will always be near and dear to my heart. Danya Ledford, also an NYU law student, came to the work later than Marisa but with a similar passion. Her adeptness for the theoretical dimensions of the book was invaluable. Jill Eisner, who studied truth and reconciliation as an NYU summer law intern in 2002, prepared an outstanding memo that became the blueprint for chapters 6 and 8 and is to be commended for her thoughtful and creative work in this area.

Leslie Glass funded Marisa, Danya, and Jill through the Leslie Glass Foundation and always supported my efforts to ask questions differently. Leslie, a successful novelist, is one of those rare popular authors who understands how to make a difference in your writing. Dottie Harris, whom I met through Leslie, played a vital role in encouraging this work to move along.

Diane Eidman of the Altria Group supported my work on domestic violence in the Jewish Orthodox community despite my reputation for troublemaking. Her courage in doing so meant that a remarkable project was funded to train six Jewish women to work sensitively and intelligently on issues of intimate abuse in the Orthodox community. Faye Zakheim, who led this effort and is remarkable in her own right, is a powerful force in my life who brings insight, joy, and excitement to this groundbreaking effort in the Jewish community. Faye knows how to get a job done and done well. Thanks to Henna White, who also works tirelessly in the Orthodox community, for her passion for my approach. Chana Widawski, Hindie Klein, and Phyllis Meyer bring their many gifts to the project and to me.

My work was catapulted into the public debate on intimate abuse when Deborah Sontag saw the merit of another point of view and appreciated the valiant efforts of people like Samuel Aymer, whom I know, and who encourages me to keep thinking differently and to remain strong. Robin Waite, so often hidden from view, was first inspired by my *Harvard Law Review* article and invited me to be the keynote speaker at the Human Resources Administration (HRA) Conference. Clearly, Deborah Sontag and Robin Waite, along with many of the participants in the HRA Conference, helped move the national consciousness beyond its mainstream thinking. A very special thanks to Leslie Grisaunti, Tara Montgomery, and especially to Oprah Winfrey, who saw the value in the debate and had the courage to air it; Resmaa, John, Christine, and the unnamed others who are doing the work—we need to give them our love and support.

So many people have touched me in ways that challenged, affirmed, or otherwise affected how I think about the vexing question of intimate abuse. They include Lonnie Athens, Bell and Paul Chevigny, Peggy Cooper Davis, Paula Fendall, Tatiana Flessas, Robert Geffner, Janet Geller, Maria Grahn-Farley, Marty Guggenheim, Christine Harrington, Carolyn Nash, Laurie Rosenblatt, and Mieko Yoshihama. Kathy Charlap and Peggy Grauwiler, both Ph.D. students at NYU's School of Social Work, encourage me to think about the policy and practice issues differently, and with the wisdom that comes with years of practice. Holly Maguigan, whose work in this area inspires me and so many others, has been a consistent presence in my evolving consciousness. Wanda Lucibello represents what prosecutors are capable of doing right.

When I decided to become Vice Provost for University Life and Interdisciplinary Initiatives in the summer of 2002, my ideas and their presentation were deeply influenced by many remarkable academic leaders. President John Sexton of NYU supported and nurtured my public work on these issues; I have learned so much from John about how to address different points of view. Provost Dave McLaughlin always encourages me to find the time to do my scholarship; Dave has been, without a doubt, the most supportive and caring colleague-supervisor with whom I have had the pleasure of working. I have truly enjoyed my travels toward academic leadership, and Dave's belief in my capacity to "do it all" has been unwavering, if not exhausting. Robert Berne provides guidance, insight, and wisdom, which I rely on much more than he knows. Yaw Nyarko and Rich Stanley have also provided support as I have faced the challenges of balancing academic and administrative life.

My very special thanks to two people who allowed me to balance the many competing demands on my time. James Rubin, a trusted friend, colleague, and administrative assistant, has always done whatever I have asked. I get great pleasure from knowing that he will begin graduate study in psychology next year. Susan Walsh, whom I have known only six months, has kept my life together as I attempt, rather clumsily, to do too many jobs at once. I literally could not manage without her intelligence, wit, and positive attitude.

My close friends and family play a very special role nurturing me through the setbacks and lunges forward. I have laughed and cried with each of them, and I am indebted to them for loving me regardless. They include Jonathan Beckenstein, Jerry Bruner, Lauren Danza, Kelly Dunn, Carol Feldman, Joel Handler, Zeke Hasenfeld, Steve Kelly Kelban, Stuart Kirk, Debra LaMorte, Duncan Lindsey, Adele Mills, Judy Mishne, Deborah Padgett, Esther Perel, Carol Prendergast, Paul Reinstein, Al Roberts, Michel Rosenfeld, Matthew Santirrocco, Jack Saul, Caty Shannon, Aja Stephan, Susan Thaler, Sharon Weinberg and Diane Yu.

Odette Botelho has been there for our son Ronnie, when I could not, with love and skill. Ellen Schall, provides unadulterated encouragement to me and sound judgment. Colleen Friend, so far away yet so close, always has the right advice. Sue Greenwald, one of my oldest best friends, persistently asks why—for this I am grateful. David Lewis, who has literally transformed his life, teaches me that unlearning violence is always possible, even for the most entrenched. And Ed Cohen, dear friend who blesses me with his art, inspires me to paint my wildest dreams.

Chuck Myers, a most remarkable editor of the old style, believed in me and my work and advocated on both counts whenever it was necessary (which was often). He understood the project at its core, and his own insight into its larger purpose improved the book significantly. I am so glad we did this one together. The reviewers who commented on the manuscript for Princeton added a great deal to its overall cohesiveness. I am especially indebted to Phyllis Goldlfarb who shared with me her acute insights into the book's meaning. Christian Purdy, Kathryn Clanton, Ellen Foos, Susan Ecklund, and everyone at Princeton University Press also helped see the book through. I am grateful to them.

Brenda Aris opened her life to me and trusted me to think about her relationship to violence. Brenda has changed how I think; she has changed me at my soul. Brenda should serve as an inspiration to us all.

My parents provide both emotional support and financial comfort. Their generosity on all counts inspires me as a human being, as a parent, and as a scholar engaged in controversy. They are truly the most remarkable parents I know.

The greatest debt is owed to the people who live with me day in and day out, and who tolerate the lows and help inspire the highs. Peter Goodrich, my lover, my partner, sits with me and writes when I am dry and lies with me when I cry. His genius is my joy, and his courage to speak his own mind, my inspiration. We do it together—this is his project as much as my own. Ronnie Goodrich, now six, reminds me of the vulnerability and instability of this and all of life's projects, and of the love that runs so deep in family dynamics. Ronnie keeps me focused on the importance of knowing my limits and seeing my own aggression.

These pages collect many of the names of people who have shared their gifts with me and who helped move me along. Whatever is left unsaid, or is said wrong, is all my own.

Linda Gayle Mills
Palm Desert, California

~ PROLOGUE

WALKING DOWN BETHNAL GREEN ROAD, AN ARTERIAL
street in working-class East London, I witnessed a remarkable scene. I
was carrying my laundry and talking with a friend when my focus was
drawn to a mother walking with her five-year-old son. He was demand-
ing attention, as all children do, and her patience suddenly snapped.
She whipped around and smacked him across the face. He staggered
backward. I was shocked that I was witnessing this violence at such
close range and simultaneously struck by its intimacy and familiarity. I
had just watched a mother assault a child in broad daylight in the middle of a crowded public street. I felt sad for the child and angry with a
mother who would treat her child this way. Before I could respond, the
child collected himself and, to my astonishment, stepped forward and
punched his mother in the stomach.

I turned and looked at my companion; we were both impressed and
somewhat pleased that the child had asserted his rights, stood up for
himself, and retaliated. Then it slowly dawned on me. In that split second, we had witnessed the genesis of intimate abuse. This was an un-
exceptional everyday scene, just another parent who felt entitled to
correct her child with physical admonitions and a child who reacted
unreflectively. But the little boy would grow up to become a man, and
he was already being taught to respond to women with violence. We
learn to become violent, as this scene suggests, but we seldom realize
that is what we are learning, let alone that it is what we are teaching.

The image of that altercation has stayed with me for many years. We all witness and experience violence in our lives. We have all become habituated to violence, consciously or unconsciously judging who is right and wrong in relation to violence. This book is, in essence, an attempt to become conscious of the pervasiveness of violence, its role in our intimate lives, and the judgments we make about it.

Becoming conscious of violence is always met with resistance. We have a hard time believing violence is occurring, even when it is direct and personal. We tend to run, either literally or metaphorically, so as to ignore it or put it behind us. Denial kicks in, and we are left pretending it never happened.

The only time we are truly comfortable thinking about violence is when it affects other people. Then we become experts on violence and on what other people should do about it. Our denial and paralysis in the face of our own experience gets externalized: we solve the problems of others while denying our own. When our anger is exteriorized in this way, it is projected: what we cannot accept in our own past, we project onto others.

Consider the reaction of a man who grew up with a violent mother. If he is unaware of his history or how it affects his view of violence, he might project his unconscious hatred of his own mother onto the woman on Bethnal Green Road. He might villainize her without any attempt to understand or engage her. Now assume he is also a social worker; he might believe that the child is best served by taking him away from his mother. It is highly unlikely that he would have any awareness that his judgment was determined, in some significant way, by his own unacknowledged prior experiences of violence.[1] When we project, we judge someone else for what happened to us; we act out our rage at our own helplessness by controlling what others do. It is a central argument of this book that to understand violence, we must attend to the "ground zero" of intimate abuse—that is, to our own experiences of it.

Returning to the five-year-old boy, it is significant that my initial response was supportive of his physical reaction to his mother's violence. I identified with the child's helplessness, with his vulnerability in the face of abuse by an adult. Most of us feel that identification when we see a child struck or otherwise abused. The reality of the situation is much more complicated. Here a mother is "coaching" a child to be abusive,[2] teaching her son to react violently toward women. I am sure we would not normally view the situation in this vein.

On reflection, what is most remarkable about this interaction is the complexity of violence between intimates; it crosses genders and generations. Unless we appreciate the dynamics of intimate abuse, we will judge it before attempting to understand it. Consider this disturbing fact: after a few years have passed and the boy who hit his mother on Bethnal Green Road has become a man, it is statistically likely that he will hit a woman again.[3] At that time, some people, especially a group called "mainstream feminists," will argue for his arrest and prosecution. What is perhaps most troubling about this situation is that mainstream feminists would at the same time leave the mother blameless. Paradoxically, mainstream feminists are arguing in this situation for the disempowerment of the violent mother and the empowerment of the violent man. The mother, viewed as a victim, is without blame. The man is the cause and the sum of the violence he inflicts. The mother's contribution to his trained reaction to women is ignored. In the most traditional of terms, he is everything, and she is nothing.

Historically, mainstream feminism's highly successful response to heterosexual domestic violence has been to ignore the complexity of the dynamic that I witnessed. The child whom I saw being hit by his mother is three times more likely to become violent in intimate relationships than a child who was not hit.[4] The moment that he hits a woman, mainstream feminists have legislated that he be taken out of the context of his biography and into an automatic legal process in which he will be held absolutely accountable for any violence he committed. He will be defined as a product of patriarchy, and his masculine privilege will account for the sole source of his aggression. For many mainstream feminists, the causal relationship between patriarchy and violence is uniform and singular; heterosexual men beat women because of patriarchy.[5] Domestic violence involves perpetrator and victim, and nothing more. While this makes for easy policy and uniform legislative solutions, it addresses the symptoms of intimate abuse and not its causes.

Mainstream feminism, a term I have drawn from others,[6] is not meant to malign any individual feminist per se. I refer to mainstream feminists as people who self-identify as "feminist" but adhere to a monolithic legal approach to domestic violence. As I will show, domestic violence does not lend itself to one solution. It is difficult to define exactly who makes up this group's membership. It may include activists, lobbyists, and helping professionals such as police officers, prosecutors, and even judges—men and women alike. Although the focus of this book is on their support for the legal process, mainstream feminists share many of the same assumptions that informed the battered women's movement early on. Many of the feminists who started and supported the battered women's movement, however, have now begun to question the decision to focus so heavily on the criminal justice system. In addition, a person may agree with aspects of the mainstream feminist approach, such as arrest, prosecution, and punishment of the most violent criminals, yet reject the rest of the mainstream agenda. In the end, mainstream feminism is a collection of ideas that a powerful group of people, with shifting membership, adhere to and advocate for. Their continued advocacy for an almost exclusive focus on punishment in response to domestic violence represents the privilege of their assertion and the positions of power they hold. It also represents, I believe, their fear that if they capitulate in any way, or recognize any limitations to their approach, they will lose the benefits they have gained.

Some people believe that calling this group of women "feminist" gives other feminists a bad name or somehow implies that there is one stereotypical feminist who supports mandated interventions. This is not the case. Many straight and gay white feminists have for a long time questioned and challenged a monolithic criminal justice response to domestic violence; many straight and gay women of color have supported mandated responses. It cannot be denied, however, that overall, mainstream feminism, as I suggest in chapter 3, has forwarded an agenda that has advanced the interests of privileged white heterosexual women at the expense of the concerns of women who are different from them, at least when it comes to criminal justice system interventions. The tensions between white feminists, women of color, and lesbians who also identify as feminists are not centered only in domestic violence. They have persisted since the feminist movement began.

This book is a reflection on where I think some feminists went wrong in relation to domestic violence and the need for other feminists to assert a different agenda. There is no one "feminism," and this book provides us with an opportunity to reflect on both our identity as feminists and what each of us stands for. Although at times it may feel like an attack—I don't mince words—it is meant to be an opportunity to see what we, as feminists, are doing and start to make deliberate decisions about the consequences of our actions.

The term "mainstream feminism" is not meant to blame any one person, but rather to point out the ways a group of feminists and their agenda have come to shape both how we think about domestic violence and what we should do about it.

I write as a feminist and activist of many year's standing. Some mainstream feminists believe my attack is fundamentally conservative in approach. As I will show, I believe the opposite is true. Conservative women have advocated that no aggressive government intervention should be made available to victims.[7] This is not my position. As a feminist, I believe that women should be entitled to their privacy to the extent that they want to maintain their privacy. If women or other members of a family want the police and/or courts to intervene, either because they ask for it or because their situation poses great risk of harm, the state should respond with appropriate assistance without reproducing the harm already being inflicted. Although in some life-threatening cases this might involve arrest, prosecution, and incarceration, in most cases a woman should be free to choose her own intimate and family destinies, with or without criminal sanctions, and after the state has provided options that respect her specific needs while also offering her methods that would help her be safe.

It is my belief, arrived at over two decades of working in the field of intimate violence, that mainstream feminists have failed to understand intimate abuse and the choices women make when they are involved in abusive relationships. To my sorrow, I have come to realize that, in general, the mainstream feminist response to domestic violence represents the views of a relatively small minority of women who have the resources and political strength to aggressively assert their narrow explanations for domestic violence. Whether by virtue of denial, projection, or privilege, mainstream feminists have been able to advocate for a uniform, and ironically conservative, law-and-order response to intimate abuse that blames men and ultimately treats women as innocent victims. Consider a recent New York City ad campaign that features pictures of men behind bars. On billboards, subway trains, and government Web sites, we see the following captions: "Successful Executive. Devoted Churchgoer. Abusive Husband." "Big Man on Campus. Star Athlete. Abusive Boyfriend." "Employee of the Month. Soccer Coach. Wife Beater." At first blush these ads seem at the very least paradoxical. If these men are successful leaders in their fields, why are they behind bars? On reflection it seems shocking that the only response available is imprisonment and shame. Can it really be asserted that their abusive behaviors are all that matter? Is it really not possible, even with successful men, to work their violence through? The mainstream law-and-order response here seems to wholly fail to address the problem; it simply wants to lock it away.

What may come as a surprise to many people is that study after study confirms that arrest, prosecution, and incarceration do not necessarily reduce the problem of domestic violence and may even be making the problem worse. Arrest has been shown to have a positive deterrent effect on men who are "good-risk" perpetrators, that is, people who have something to lose by being incarcerated.[8] On the other hand, the men most likely to be arrested because of the criminal justice system's inherent class and race bias can become more violent in response to arrest.[9] Even a coordinated response that includes arrest, prosecution, and incarceration has not shown better outcomes. Although there are conflicting results, no study documents an overwhelming reduction in intimate violence in the groups most likely to be arrested.[10] At worst, the criminal justice system increases violence against women. At best, it has little or no effect.

The assumptions underpinning mainstream feminist advocacy efforts are that all intimate abuse is heterosexual, that violence is a one-way street (male to female), that all violence warrants a state response, and that women want to leave rather than stay in their abusive relationships. It is on this basis that mainstream feminists advocated for interventions that called for the state to arrest and prosecute batterers regardless of the woman's wishes. Mandatory arrest and prosecution, as they have come to be called, became the battle cry of mainstream feminists. Their efforts were overwhelmingly successful.

Their success was important and drastically lowered the level of social tolerance for domestic violence and focused attention on the pervasiveness and danger of intimate abuse. Their success, no doubt, immobilized some men who were so violent that they would otherwise have killed their intimate partners. It is important however, to distinguish between that end of the spectrum that sociologist Michael Johnson dubs "patriarchal terrorism," and "common couple violence," which reflects the more common dynamic I describe throughout this book.[11] My argument is that recognizing that some men inflict severe physical and emotional violence on women is important, but in many cases it is neither the whole story of violence in that relationship, nor the most common instance of violence in the intimate sphere.

Here is the history. Thirty years ago, law enforcement personnel paid no attention to domestic violence and certainly did not listen to women's complaints. Twenty years ago, women, some of whom had left their abusers, started shelters and assumed that the women who came for safety or a respite from the violence ultimately needed to leave their abusive relationships. They called these battered women "victims." The irony is that statistics reflected the fact that many of these women stayed and/or returned to their abusers.[12] Yet shelter workers were politically motivated and did not stop to listen to the women who said that they sought only temporary refuge, that they were returning to their abusers.[13] Women in abusive relationships remained unheard.

Ten years ago, mainstream feminists successfully advocated for policies that instituted mandatory arrest, prosecution, and reporting even though there was evidence that such action may increase the incidence of violence against poor women of color. As Lawrence Sherman and his colleagues observed after studying mandatory arrest practices in the city of Milwaukee: "If three times as many blacks as whites are arrested, which is a fair approximation, then an across-the-board policy of mandatory arrest prevents 2,504 acts of violence against primarily white women at the price of 5,409 acts of violence against primarily black women."[14] Because arrest in Milwaukee is more likely to prevent future violence when the batterer is white, mandatory arrests protect the partners of white men, who are most often white women, while threatening the partners of black men, who are predominantly black women. And since three times as many black men are arrested as white men, partners of black men are at a disproportionately increased risk.

Simultaneously, mainstream feminist theory sought to explain violence against women by linking it to male oppression. After a relentless and successful effort, these feminist explanations took hold, and many men's and women's narratives of intimate violence incorporated notions of patriarchy into their explanations of it. The feminist strategy to construct domestic violence as a gender issue has worked. A natural consequence of this consciousness is that mainstream feminists decided that the government should no longer collude with batterers in legitimizing violence against women. Through concerted advocacy efforts, the mainstream feminist movement persuaded the state to acknowledge the oppression of women in the intimate sphere and to legislate that men's violence against women should never be tolerated.

This history is distinctive for another important reason. People were so concerned about promoting a universal explanation for violence against women that nobody listened to the people involved in abusive relationships, and, in consequence, nobody knows how to listen. There is neither a methodology for listening nor any space within which to attend to women's and men's stories. Years of research, which mainstream feminism has glossed over or ignored, shows that when it comes to intimate abuse, women are far from powerless and seldom, if ever, just victims. Women are not merely passive prisoners of violent intimate dynamics. Like men, women are frequently aggressive in intimate settings and therefore may be more accurately referred to as "women in abusive relationships" (a term I prefer to the more common usages "battered women," "victim," or "survivor").

The studies show not only that women stay in abusive relationships but also that they are intimately engaged in and part of the dynamic of abuse.[15] As the studies of lesbian violence demonstrate,[16] women are capable of being as violent as men in intimate relationships. And women can be physically violent as well as emotionally abusive.[17] That violence comes out in their intimate relationships both as resistance and as aggression. We need to put aside our preconceptions of gender socialization and roles. Women are abusive in all forms and expressions in the intimate sphere, and it is up to feminists to do something about it.

What is appallingly apparent is that we have refused to address the role of women in the dynamic of intimate violence. The reasons for this are numerous. Perhaps the most important is that some feminists fear that talking about and addressing these issues reinforces the stereotypical assumption that women are somehow to blame for the abuse inflicted on them. In my view, the research on women's violence and the numerous studies that have clearly indicated that women are no less physically violent or emotionally abusive toward men than are men toward women creates an opportunity. It allows us to address women's responsibility in the dynamic of abuse without blaming them for the violence inflicted back.[18] Although we do not know exactly what female violence expresses (mainstream feminists have argued it is always defensive), or what it means politically or even intimately, we should realize that women are participating to one degree or another in a dynamic of abuse, and hence are stronger and more resilient than we think. Seeing that intimate violence involves so much more than men's violence against women, acknowledging that it involves a dynamic between couples, is thus a feminist issue.

Once we recognize intimate abuse as a dynamic, we can become more accepting of certain of its often inevitable features. Women stay in abusive relationships whether we approve or not. Studies have shown that half of women return to their abusive partners after they are discharged from a shelter.[19] Women stay in violent and abusive intimate relationships for emotional, familial, cultural, religious, and economic reasons. They stay because they have an intimate relationship with and emotional attachment to their partners, their children, and the life they have built.[20] For better or worse, their staying shows at least some resilience and strength, an ability to negotiate and to remain attached.[21] Seeing staying in an abusive relationship as more than just women's socialization within a patriarchal system is an important starting point for interrupting violence. This fact has been denied by mainstream feminists.

It has served mainstream feminism both socially and politically to simplify and reduce the violence continuum to include only physical abuse perpetrated by men. Mainstream feminists made domestic violence unilateral. A violence that was a facet of a family or domestic scene was portrayed as an inevitable, if unfortunate, expression of patriarchy. The reason that I label domestic violence as "intimate abuse" is precisely to draw attention to the crucial fact that intimate violence is intimate, a product of intimacy and an expression of relationship. Intimate abuse is a mode, however failing, of communication between lovers, friends, and family members, and not just between a mythologized patriarch and an innocent woman.

In the first part of this book, I reflect on and rethink intimate abuse. In chapter 1, I begin to explore the pervasiveness of violence in our lives, and how we have been socialized to look away from violence and to judge it from a distance. From this perspective, I introduce the mainstream feminist response to domestic violence and expose the four assumptions that have affected how we have been influenced to think about it. I challenge these assumptions with the needs, desires, and perspectives of women who are abused. This involves going to the ground zero of intimate abuse. Using the case of Monique and Jim Brown, I expose how little we listen to and acknowledge what women say they experience and what they say they desire for their intimate relationships, even when they are abusive. Mainstream feminists will frequently ignore things they do not wish to hear and override them with assumptions of which even they may not be conscious. We need to make our judgments about intimate abuse conscious and we need to attend to the origins of those judgments—our own lives. The argument drawn from looking inward is simple and powerful and sets the stage for rethinking our preconceptions both about violence and about the appropriate political, legal, and therapeutic responses to it.

Chapter 2 presents evidence that there is limited empirical support for the assumption that mandatory arrest and prosecution policies in domestic violence cases have the intended effect of reducing violence against women. A review of the literature exposes how these strategies can actually increase incidents of intimate abuse against certain women. Factors such as race, education, and employment all influence whether mandated arrest and prosecution policies increase or decrease violence. In addition to being ineffective in these ways, these policies rob women in abusive relationships of their personal power, with the devastating long-term effect of inadvertently diminishing women's capacity to reduce the violence they are experiencing.

Chapter 3 exposes the power dynamics behind mandatory policies and the ways mainstream feminists and the professionals who carry out these policies exert power over the women they claim to help. The irony is that when women in abusive relationships feel a modicum of control or personal power, incidents of violence against them decrease.[22] The question is: If we know that women who perceive that they have control in their abusive relationships can have an effect on the violence they are experiencing, why have mainstream feminists advocated for policies that undermine that sense of control? Countertransference, the personal reactions of mainstream feminists and professionals to their clients' stories based on their own histories of abuse, may help answer this question. Mainstream feminists' lack of reflection on their own histories limited their capacity to encourage a more empowering approach. They developed such theories as learned helplessness and trauma to define how to think about intimate abuse, instead of presenting a more complete picture of a woman in an abusive relationship influenced not only by patriarchy but by culture, race, religion, and emotional attachment. I argue that mainstream feminism has not done the self-reflection necessary to understand these complexities and that it desperately needs to do so to understand how mandated policies can damage women in abusive relationships both emotionally and physically.

Chapter 4 questions the assumption that only men can be violent and that male violence is the only form of aggression that should be recognized as important. The assumption that violence is distinctly male and physical was a deliberate strategy of mainstream feminists who undertook the task of criminalizing intimate abuse. The irony is that these feminists colluded in dismissing women yet again. Rather than recognizing that women were also physically violent and played a significant role in the dynamic of intimate violence, mainstream feminists dismissed and discounted female violence as insufficiently visible and strong. They also excluded female emotional abuse and aggression from the assessment of violence, and this despite the fact that it was intimate violence that was being addressed. Yet violence is ubiquitous and operates along a continuum that includes emotional abuse, shouting, and hitting, as well as strangling or shooting. We all experience violence in our intimate or family lives. Drawing on the case of Brenda Aris, a battered woman from California who shot her sleeping husband, we learn the extent to which women can react violently and also how much we seek to deny this reality. Projection, as one form of countertransference, helps us understand how mainstream feminists have narrowed intimate abuse to serve their political and social goals. By projecting onto men the aggression they reject in themselves, or explaining away the violence expressed by women like Brenda Aris as exclusively defensive, mainstream feminism has succeeded in repressing the ways women's aggression may be contributing to the intimate abuse dynamic. This only serves to reinforce our denial of the presence of intimate and family violence in each of our lives, a fact we must reckon with if we ever hope to address it.

In the second part of the book, I develop a method to fix the failures of past approaches. In chapter 5, I present support for my argument that violence is a dynamic between people that must be recognized if we are serious about addressing it. This involves becoming conscious of the intimate abuse in each of our lives and the ways we have responded to it so as to better ensure that our reaction to other people's violence is more thoughtful, as opposed to the projection and countertransference that currently inform our judgments about these issues.

This larger understanding of intimate violence clarifies how the dynamic of abuse occurs and how victims, such as children, learn to become violent through their early exposure to aggression. The violence can become particularly acute when couples get together and attachment styles developed in childhood are revealed. At the heart of the dynamic of abuse is the important fact that all violence matters, physical and emotional, male and female, heterosexual and homosexual, parent and child, and that a feminist paradigm of intimate abuse should recognize this reality.

In chapters 6 and 7, I develop specific approaches and strategies for professionals and laypeople alike to relate to heterogeneous groups of people in abusive relationships, both men and women, heterosexual and homosexual, white and of color. In chapter 6, I introduce, as an alternative to the criminal justice system, Intimate Abuse Circles. These circles, drawn from restorative justice models and developed out of the South African experience of Truth and Reconcilation, recognize the importance of the abusive dynamic and provide a forum for addressing it. Depending on the extent of violence and the desires of the couple, these circles involve both parties and a care community (family, friends, clergy, etc.) who participate in a process of recognition, responsibility, and change. Learning to recognize and take responsibility for one's contribution to a dynamic is key to interrupting its transmission.

In chapter 7, I present a method for listening in the Intimate Abuse Circles that is respectful of both parties involved in the dynamic. This approach is in keeping with the research that suggests that men become less violent and women more empowered when each feels respected and heard by the professionals and care communities who are expected to help them.[23] Chapter 8 concludes with evidence that suggests that restorative justice models, on which the Intimate Abuse Circles are designed, have had remarkable success in reducing incidents of violence. Their effects are sure to ripple beyond the men and women who participate in them, to other family members and to future generations.

This book is very much a part of a larger feminist effort to understand and reempower women to address violence. Our culture hopes that we can ignore or simplify violence and that it will go away. Mainstream feminists have unwittingly colluded in this thinking by hoping to end violence while ignoring its complexities. The war on drugs gets repeated in a war on violence and with similarly nugatory effects. Just as attempting to eradicate drugs without understanding their appeal tends to preclude both insight and effective policies in reducing their use, attempting to obliterate intimate violence without understanding it may increase the violence rather than reduce it. It is the intellectual equivalent of sweeping it under the carpet. The war on drugs says that if we lock up drug dealers, we will end demand; the war on violence says that if we lock up all the men who abuse women, then intimate violence will end. This does not recognize the violence of the policy itself, the aggression embedded in each of us, or the indisputable empirical fact that many of those incarcerated without treatment will be released and will offend again. As we will see, obliterating the symptoms does not cure the causes.

Consider a miscellany of recent instances of this logic. A study reports that women who have abortions suffer horribly because they are prevented from expressing their loss. The political struggle for the right to abortion has been taken as an unchallengeable reason for denying any negative side effects for fear that they may enhance the arguments of pro-life advocates.[24] In another instance, an Australian billiards star was charged with rape in England after a highly ambivalent late-night sexual encounter.[25] The complainant woman admitted that she undressed and straddled him naked but later claimed that she did not consent to penetration by the penis. It has to be acknowledged or at least canvassed, even by feminists, that her "no" could have been a teasing "yes." Another article from a British newspaper reports that a clinic for treatment of child abusers was closed after residents protested against having a treatment program in their vicinity.[26] The tragedy is that the abstract desire to eliminate child abuse actually prevents any real effort to do so.

These examples share a common structure. In each case, a traumatic event leads to a community fleeing the trauma itself. Those involved transfer, externalize, or project the trauma. When certain feminists fear the loss of the right to abortion, they deny women who have had abortions the space to talk about them. When these same feminists fear the law's recalcitrance in relation to rape charges, they deny that a woman can say no ambivalently. When a community fears child abuse, it cannot tolerate the presence of child abusers even if their presence is the precondition of a cure. Time and again, and these are just a few recent examples, we see that it is easier in the short term to turn away from violence than it is to face up to it. The same is true of intimate abuse; as I will show, it affects us all in one way or another—whether we turn away from it or not. I am suggesting that by looking at it directly, we can at least become conscious of the ways we want to look away and what is lost, in terms of cure, when we do so.

It is our experience of violence that both informs our response and triggers our panic or prejudgments. This book underscores the importance of being in the presence of violence and acknowledging its proximity both to us and to others. The lesson is that only by looking at the violence—its complexity, its history, its tendrils throughout our culture—can we begin to understand, address, and ameliorate our relationship to it.

I believe that although on the surface a lot has changed in relation to intimate abuse over the last thirty years, the work has largely focused on casting the abuse as violence against women. Although in some instances this accurately characterizes the phenomenon, it is far from the whole story. Recognizing that we all have narratives of intimate abuse and corresponding experiences with violence partly explains why we have responded so vehemently to the problem. This recognition provides a starting point for a more informed and less judgmental practice. It also provides an opportunity to rethink the limitations of our current strategies and to reformulate our current theories of intimate abuse.

It is the key argument of this book that the history of feminist responses to intimate abuse has precluded any adequate understanding of the complexity and intimacy of violence in domestic relationships. Yet developing an adequate feminist theory is the most practical of current tasks. To understand violence we need to situate ourselves in relation to it and acknowledge, reflect on, and work through those aspects of our experiences that get replicated in our judgment of violence in others. It is striking and shocking that the violence that I witnessed on Bethnal Green Road was the violence of a mother against a child, female against male, and one generation against the next. We face a choice: either, as historically has happened, we can prejudge this violence and so turn away and run from it. Or, as chapter 1 elaborates, we can walk toward the violence and endeavor to understand and work through it.

Everything is at stake. The boy will become a man, and another generation's relationship to violence will be defined. His mother will be exonerated, and his wife will be labeled a victim. His children might be the recipients of his or even her violence, and/or might become violent themselves. No one will seize the opportunity offered, each time intimate abuse occurs, to stop and reflect on the violence and, as I am suggesting, seize the chance to do something about it.

PART ONE

Rethinking Our Responses
to Intimate Abuse

ONE

The Ground Zero of Intimate Abuse

THERE IS A STRIKING SIMILARITY BETWEEN HOW WE AS A nation react to such mass violence as September 11 and how we individually and collectively respond to intimate abuse. The experiences of my lower Manhattan neighborhood help illuminate those similarities. On September 11, 2001, Ronnie, my five-year-old son, was a kindergarten student at P.S. 234, an elementary school that is located a few blocks from the World Trade Center. After the attack, the 640 children who attended the school were displaced for more than six months, and two alternative sites were used as classrooms while the parents debated the safety of returning to the school.

In the months immediately following the attacks, the debate focused on air quality. Some parents believed that we were literally killing our children if we exposed them to the dust generated by Ground Zero's recovery effort. I believed the problem was more than just the physical environment; it was also our emotional ties to it. Parent meetings only confirmed my belief. The topic of air quality was so infused with emotion, with words of life and death, that I was sure that there was much more, emotionally speaking, to the business of returning than the parents were articulating.

I wanted the kids to reoccupy P.S. 234 as soon after the event as was physically possible. The trauma literature unequivocally provides that children recover more quickly from disasters if they resume as "normal" a routine as soon as possible. The longer it takes for them to do so, the more likely they are to experience post-traumatic stress disorder.[1] After a long struggle and the passage of five months, a majority of parents finally felt it was safe enough to reoccupy the P.S. 234 building.

After returning to the building, I attended a meeting that was slightly different from previous gatherings. Several parents had been monitoring the air quality since moving back to the school. As I had anticipated, the air was fine. Although some parents still believed the windows should remain closed, they could no longer claim that Ground Zero posed a treacherous health hazard. The business of our children's mental health was clearly the only thing left on the agenda.

Organized by the school psychologist, Bruce Arnold, the meeting in the school library began with bagels and coffee. (Feeding the parents at meetings such as these had become a ritual as we moved from location to location in search of a safe haven.) Dr. Arnold began by reporting that the survey filled out by parents of pre-K students and first graders confirmed that since returning to the P.S. 234 building, 90 percent of these young children were doing "good" to "very good." These results were consistent with the teachers' impressions; 90 percent of the teachers felt that the youngest children in the school were doing "good" to "very good."

After Arnold's presentation, the parents started to share their own impressions. As at the meetings I had previously attended, although the parents would report that their kids were doing well, they themselves remained full of anxiety. I was relieved to hear that these parents were finally acknowledging their own mental health concerns, but I was nervous that many of them were transferring to their children their fears that another terrorist attack *on them* was still imminent.

One mother described how her parents, who live out of town, wanted to take her six-year-old daughter to a movie on a Saturday afternoon. The mom refused. When her parents pressed, she became angry: "What if something happened? You wouldn't know what to do. You wouldn't know how to get to me." An attempt to exert control, the little we have, can be a feature of trauma recovery.[2]

Several parents described how they had stopped watching television or listening to the radio; they believed this protected their children from knowing that threats of terrorism continued. This reminded me of a meeting with parents a few weeks after the World Trade Center attacks where some people had suggested that the kids and the teachers be prohibited from talking about what they saw. Some parents had never told their children what happened on September 11, and they did not want other kids telling them the truth. The truth is that on that day, nearly every child and many parents at P.S. 234 ran for their lives—myself, my husband, and my son included.

At this most recent meeting, several parents described their ongoing startle response, their hypervigilance to sounds or visuals. When a loud noise from a garbage truck filtered through the closed windows in the library where we were sitting, a frightened chill passed across each of our faces. You could see that some parents acknowledged it and moved on. Others remained tense. These moments mattered. Escalating or de-escalating the effect of such sounds on the psyche is one of the primary tasks of the person affected by trauma.[3] It is especially important that parents learn to manage their fear so as to minimize passing it on to their children—even in the face of ongoing threats.[4]

As the meeting was winding down, one mother told a different kind of story. Her five-year-old daughter, Sara, had been terrified of fires after September 11.[5] She said that each time the phone rang, Sara thought that someone was calling to tell them that their home was on fire. This mother was very perplexed by her daughter's response. She would attempt to calm Sara by stating that everything was fine. Despite this ongoing reassurance, however, Sara continued to harbor anxiety.

One day, the little girl expressed her anxiety about fire again, and the mother heard Sara differently. She started to hear that her own parental denial and reassurances were not working, and she started to think more critically about how to help Sara recover. She considered that not talking about what happened only made it loom larger and scarier in her daughter's mind.

The mother took Sara to the local fire station and told the firefighters that her daughter was afraid of fire. The local fire captain described how he would be there to help if any fires got started and the methods he had at his disposal. Then the mother visited Saint Vincent's Hospital and showed Sara the ambulances that lined the streets "just in case."

Finally, she took her daughter to the World Trade Center site to explore how such a tragedy occurred and why so many people survived. She explained the recovery effort and the journey involved in healing. By the end of the week, Sara was less anxious. Her mother, too, had come to accept what had happened and could talk about it, and Sara could rest at night. Trauma can be contradictory and counterintuitive in that way. The nature of trauma is that the event is always close to the surface, whether remembered or forgotten. In addition, what a person seems to need—to divert his or her mind from the events—may be just the opposite of what he or she really needs. Healing from trauma is aided by both returning to one's routine and immersing oneself in what happened for the specific purpose of working through the painful events.[6]

There is never the question of eradicating violence. Violence is ubiquitous, touching each of our lives. The issue is not whether we can avoid it but rather what we do with our experiences of it. That is what the attacks of September 11 and all our violent experiences can teach us.

This mother's initial response to September 11, as well as those of the other parents I described, parallels a typical response to violence. We pretend it did not happen, we reassure ourselves (and our children) it was an isolated event, or we obsess about our helplessness or fear in relation to it. We try to exert control over the violence by being afraid of it or otherwise denying it. We do not make efforts to understand it; we simply fear, avoid, or deny it. What is clearly true is that we have no language for the violence. We have no words to put to it. We have only our memory to share or deny. If we share it and seek to learn more about it, we can recover. If we repress it, our worlds become restricted. We don't go to movies; we don't open our windows; we don't talk.

Violence is paradoxical. One would think that telling a child that the events of September 11 were an isolated incident would provide comfort. That may be true of some children. However, other children are comforted by a full airing of the facts. Like adults, children usually learn to manage their anxiety most effectively with reassurance through information rather than with silence, distortion, or unexplored fear.

Terrorist violence is not the only violence we have been exposed to.

Those who acknowledge violence see it everywhere. It is in our intimate lives; it is in our community lives. It is in our children's lives and our parents' lives. Coming to terms with the ubiquity of violence is necessary in order for us to understand it and take the necessary steps to recognize and respond to it with awareness—and eventually to heal from it.

I think of violence broadly. I think it exists along a continuum that includes emotional, financial, physical, and sexual violence. The continuum of violence is unique to each person. To some, emotional abuse is more severe than sexual abuse. To others, sexual abuse is the ultimate human violation. All of us have had the experience of overhearing how others treat each other. Some are horrified by the slightest raised voice; to others, a slap is friendly family banter. When we are reflective, each of us knows when a push *feels* part of friendly play or *feels* coercive. The problem is that what feels playful or not *to us* may or may not parallel what *feels* abusive to others. If we do not create a language for discussing these issues, or an opportunity to learn more about each other's relationship to abuse, we will continue to misjudge and misunderstand intimate violence as isolated events that come out of nowhere.

My premise is that we have all experienced intimate violence, which in turn is what affects our relationship to it. In the classes where I teach this, most students at first resist this broad characterization. By the end of the semester, though, each person has recounted at least one personal story in which he or she was emotionally and/or physically abused. Sometimes it is more difficult to recount a story if one was aggressive or the abuser; it is easier to see another person as the aggressor. But in time, those stories come, too. Through this history, my students learn more about how they react to violence and why; they can begin to be more reflective about it.

I propose that intimate violence is a part of all our lives. Coming to this realization parallels the process the mother went through with her daughter's anxiety about fires. At first she denied it—understandably so. It did not happen to her. It happened to other people. In time, the child triggered a more thoughtful response in the mother. When we think of intimate violence, we try to believe that our views about it and reactions to it are outside of ourselves. Our responses to intimate violence, we believe, are based on other people's lives, triggered by situations that are worse than our own and victims more helpless than we are. Our responses are about anything but ourselves.

What we will find if we go deeper is that by visiting the ground zero of intimate abuse, we can see the path from which our opinions about intimate abuse are formulated: O. J. and Nicole Simpson, Jim and Monique Brown, the Menendez brothers—each of these cases generated within us a narrative—a story about what happened or should have happened. I suggest that the genesis of these deep feelings is our own lives, our own unexplored histories and experiences with intimate abuse, along with cultural influences, including mainstream feminist thinking and the media, that help shape that narrative. Uncovering these hidden influences suddenly frees us to move beyond our narrow explanations for violence, as well as our narrow solutions to it.

A TYPICAL STORY

Mainstream feminists have spent the last thirty years convincing us that their interpretation of intimate abuse as a result of patriarchy should be ours. This interpretation has been powerful and influential, and it now dominates how the state views domestic violence and responds to it. But does it serve the people in violent relationships? I believe that the now-hegemonic interpretation, meant to help women in abusive relationships, paradoxically hurts them. To show how, I offer a typical, though celebrated, intimate abuse case.

In September 1999, Jim Brown was prosecuted in Los Angeles for breaking the windows on his wife's car and threatening to kill her. He had been charged with misdemeanor spousal abuse after Monique Brown called 911 from a neighbor's house, reporting to detectives that her husband had threatened to "kill her" by "snapping her neck."[7]

Several weeks after Jim Brown's initial arrest, Monique Brown told a different story about what happened that night. She told the public and later a jury that her husband had not threatened her. She told a surprised nation that she had called 911 to punish Jim Brown because she believed he "was having an affair."[8]

The only thing that makes the Brown case different from the thousands of misdemeanor domestic violence cases prosecuted in the United States each year is that Jim Brown is a member of the Pro Football and College Football Halls of Fame. The story was carried in every major newspaper and reported on all the morning and evening news shows. But despite the nation's attention, Monique Brown acted like most victims of domestic violence. She told a different story to the jury than the one she told the 911 operator on the night of the alleged attack. She revised her story when the criminal justice system decided to prosecute and incarcerate the man she loved. When push came to shove, Monique Brown chose to protect her relationship with her husband rather than ally herself with the state that sought to punish him.

Mandatory arrest, prosecution, and reporting policies dictate that police officers, prosecutors, and even medical personnel should proceed against the batterer by arresting, prosecuting, or reporting him regardless of the battered woman's wishes. Many police officers and prosecutors complain that these stringent policies against domestic violence—a dramatic and seemingly necessary development in the past twenty years—have not produced victims who are more willing to press charges against their batterers. A majority of prosecutors find that over 55 percent of the victims they represent are "uncooperative" as they attempt to indict and incarcerate the batterers.[9] Physicians fail to report domestic violence allegations for fear that they will not be able to manage the needs or demands of their patients once a report is made.[10]

An insight can help explain why women are ambivalent about engaging with the criminal justice system. Two decades ago, battered women were not consulted on whether the batterer should be arrested; with mandatory policies, their points of view on these matters are still considered largely irrelevant. Instead, women in abusive relationships are placed in the untenable position of choosing between protecting their lovers or husbands from incarceration or protecting themselves by relying on a criminal justice system that is unresponsive to their individual needs.[11]

Jim Brown's wife, Monique, journeyed through the criminal justice system and faced all the challenges and paradoxes of a mandatory system. Mrs. Brown had two options: she could protect herself by testifying against her husband, or she could protect her husband by not testifying against him. Mrs. Brown made the decision most women make: she chose to protect her husband. By doing this, she rendered ineffective the prosecutor's efforts to hold Jim Brown responsible for the domestic violence crimes he had allegedly committed. Jim Brown was eventually acquitted of "threatening to kill" his wife and therefore convicted of a less significant crime.[12] It was Los Angeles's mandatory prosecution policy that helped Brown escape these more serious charges. Through these policies, the prosecutor was forced to bring the case to trial, rather than to find a middle ground with Monique Brown that may have held her husband more accountable for the intimate violence he committed in ways that addressed the violence rather than judged it.

My position is that Los Angeles's unreflective mandatory prosecution policy placed Monique Brown in the untenable position of choosing between her own safety and her husband's freedom. Rather than helping Monique and Jim Brown to understand and address the violence and related dynamics in their relationship, this policy had the exclusive goal of punishing Jim Brown. Because this was incompatible with Monique Brown's desires, her only option was to protect her abusive husband from incarceration.

The problem in the Brown case started even before the prosecutor's office entered the picture. Rather than heeding Monique Brown's request to 911 that the police help her "fix her troubled marriage," they arrived with "shotguns, bulletproof vests, and cold stares."[13] By ignoring Monique Brown's stated desires, and pursuing a criminal prosecution instead, the state's representatives not only alienated Mrs. Brown from the helping professionals she needed but actually sent her toward her husband's abuse. Finally, by discounting Mrs. Brown's belief that Jim Brown's violent reaction was potentially related to her jealous rage, the state deprived Mrs. Brown of an opportunity to discover the ways she could understand and perhaps take some responsibility for their violent dynamic without assuming blame for his violence. My argument is that if the state were to develop insight into the dynamics of intimate abuse, it could help women like Mrs. Brown be reflective about or reject the dynamics in their intimate relationships, rather than reproducing them.

To develop this insight, we must move toward an understanding of the violence, much as Sara had to get nearer to the realities of September 11 to reconcile herself with them.

THE MAINSTREAM FEMINIST RESPONSE
TO DOMESTIC VIOLENCE

The paradoxes of the Jim and Monique Brown case illustrate the flaws in the mainstream feminist approach to intimate violence. One glove does not fit all hands; mandatory policies do not suit all relationships or all incidents of intimate abuse. Yet mainstream feminists insist these policies are the best solution to abuse. If we want to understand the limitations of these policies, we must first understand the assumptions that ground the mainstream feminist narrative of domestic violence.

The first assumption of mainstream feminists is that men batter women because our patriarchal society permits them to do so. Men batter women because men, as patriarchs, are privileged physically, financially, and socially. These circumstances create the conditions under which men like Jim Brown are given permission to beat women. Men's violence against women is a holdover from previous generations when men owned women as property and could treat "it" as such.[14] Given this overriding, deep, and historical threat to women, men's violence must be met with a vigorous and vehement response by the criminal justice system. Anything short of incarceration is inadequate. Implicit in this assumption is the belief that we need not attempt to understand men's violence beyond the patriarchal explanation provided.

A second and correlative assumption is that women stay in abusive relationships because of patriarchy. They fear their abusers and lack the material resources to leave. Women who stay do so out of weakness, lack of consciousness, and an inability to act decisively by leaving. If given the appropriate political, financial, legal, and emotional support, women would always choose to leave their abusive partners.[15]

The third assumption is that the criminal justice system is sexist. Police officers, prosecutors, and judges minimize the problem of domestic violence, deny women agency, and discredit women's accounts of their abuse. Mainstream feminists say that society has tolerated men's violence against their intimate partners for too long. Although society does not tolerate male-on-male violence, stranger violence, or other forms of public violence, it still tolerates violence by men against their female intimate partners.[16]

The fourth assumption is that only extraordinary measures will counteract men's patriarchal power and violence, women's weakness, and the justice system's sexism. Specifically, it is assumed that the history of denial justifies treating all domestic violence as the equivalent of violence between strangers. Mandatory measures are necessary to overcome the state's sexism and men's hopeless violence. In this view, it follows that jail or prison terms are the only appropriate response to intimate abuse.

These assumptions have come to form the ideological foundations of American domestic violence practice and policy making. The extent to which they have been integrated into our routine thinking represents the success of the mainstream feminist movement over the past thirty years. The movement has persuaded citizen and lawmaker alike of the indisputable veracity of these assumptions, which are so significant to the movement to end violence against women that they have become markers for feminism. As they have become so deeply ingrained in our political culture, few have questioned them. If you do question them, you have abandoned the movement. Yet these tenets need to be questioned.

Each assumption can be challenged on the basis of recent work in social, cultural, and gender studies. And in the past fifteen years, diverse groups have begun reconsidering these assumptions. These groups include men and women of color; scholars of sociology, psychology, and psychoanalysis; ethnic, racial, and religious groups; advocacy organizations; and the very men and women who are involved in violent relationships. These groups have shown that mainstream feminists have formulated a definition of intimate abuse that has largely disregarded the emotional, racial, ethnic, and religious dynamics of that violence.

Let us return to the first assumption that underpins mandatory policies: domestic violence is caused by and restricted to patriarchal governance. This, however, is neither a universal truth nor necessarily the best explanation of intimate abuse across cultures. For example, men and women of color often do not agree with the dominant rhetoric that all men are "patriarchs." Indeed, many women and men of color see the white power structure as representing the views of a patriarch who oppresses not only women but also communities of color. Lesbians, gays, bisexual, and transgendered people often find mainstream explanations of intimate violence completely irrelevant to their experiences of violence.[17] For women who choose a religious lifestyle, patriarchy is a foreign and irrelevant concept. Similarly, immigrant women steeped in traditional cultural values do not identify their experiences of violence with patriarchy. Their explanations include the realities of their lives: the difficult migration challenges that their families, and especially their husbands, often face. Women, like Monique Brown, who love their husbands, may not respond to a condemnation of these men as patriarchs. Although patriarchy may have helped shape the dynamic in these relationships, conversations with each of these people must begin with their own perspectives. In this book, I seek to challenge mainstream feminism's narrow conception of intimate abuse as patriarchy and provide a methodology for incorporating a multiplicity of voices affected by intimate violence.

If we blame patriarchy for abuse, then we believe that only men abuse women, that women do not abuse men. But violence is never that simple. As I have already suggested, empirical research supports the assertion that men and women often abuse each other.[18] There is no doubt that injury is a distinct feature of men's violence against women that requires our attention, a topic I discuss in more detail in chapter 6. But even though the research confirms that men are much more likely to injure their female partners visibly, this simply points to the most obvious, least subtle manifestation of abuse.[19] In addition, men, in general, minimize women's violence and, as such, are less likely to identify it as abuse.[20] On the other hand, women are much more likely to identify any aggressive action by their male partner as violent.[21] Finally, we can add that mainstream feminist thought has a history of ignoring the unique dynamics of abuse in gay and lesbian relationships. In truth, the fact that violence exists in gay and lesbian relationships threatens the core tenet that men abuse women because patriarchy encourages them to do so.

Factors other than patriarchy may explain the prevalence of intimate abuse across genders and sexual orientations. We have already learned that a child (whether male or female) who experienced violence is three times more likely to become violent in adult intimate relationships than a child who was not hit.[22] Similarly, studies indicate that men who grew up with mothers who were excessively critical are much more likely to abuse their intimate partners in adulthood.[23] Both these facts raise questions about children who are exposed to intimate abuse and its attending implications. This is a distinct and important issue, which I address peripherally in my explanations of the origins of violence in chapter 5. These facts also expose the reality that a mother may retaliate against her children for her husband's abuse. Even if this is true, such behavior toward children should not be excused. As we will see very clearly in chapter 4, intimate abuse will cross gender and generational lines, and regardless of its origins, it will continue to plague men and women alike until the pattern is interrupted.

The second structuring assumption—that women stay in abusive relationships out of weakness, fear, or lack of adequate feminist consciousness—has also been challenged. Many women remain in violent relationships. The women who eventually terminate their relationships will likely return to the men abusing them many times before leaving permanently.[24] In all cases, women try desperately to decide what to do. They are deeply conflicted about how to address the abuse while trying to preserve what they value in their relationships. Some advocates and scholars believe that focusing on the woman's return draws our attention away from the batterer's abuse. But *not* to focus on the return neglects women's voices and concerns. The woman whose voice needs to be heard may be in an abusive relationship, but she is also quite possibly a mother, a lover, a friend, a family member, or part of a church or a tradition that has competing claims upon her decisions. In addition, if, as I have just suggested, intimate abuse cannot be defined simply as a man beating a woman, it is not always clear who is the victim, who ought to leave. Understanding these dynamics helps us help women in violent relationships. It also helps us understand domestic violence more intimately—from each party's point of view—rather than reacting without listening to their stories.

The final assumption made by mainstream feminists is that the criminal justice system has for years treated intimate abuse in a sexist manner by overlooking it, and that this justifies a homogeneous and extreme—perhaps even violent—response now. Although it is true that violence between intimate partners has been systematically overlooked by the criminal justice system, we should not assume that it should be treated like stranger violence, which is distinctly different. When we do not know the perpetrator of the violence, it is relatively easy psychologically to criminalize his or her acts. Criminalizing intimate abuse on a model that has been derived from stranger violence ignores the intimate nature of the crime. It ignores the fact that the parties to the crime have children together or they share the experience of marginalization through migration, race, or sexual orientation. Violence that occurs in an intimate relationship is not conducive to a paradigm that assigns all the blame to one party while wholly exonerating the other. This expropriation, coupled with the idea that intimate violence is best addressed by silencing the victim and letting the state take the initiative against the batterer, ignores the significance of a woman's agency when she is threatened by intimate violence. This is not to say that women who want to separate from their partners because of abuse should not be permitted or even encouraged to do so. Rather, the road to reducing violence overall involves recognizing its influence and effect on all parties and encouraging dialogue about it.

Finally, and perhaps most strikingly, by criminalizing domestic violence, the racism that is endemic to the criminal justice system is underscored. Men of color are likely to be arrested and prosecuted for intimate abuse crimes at disturbingly disproportionate rates when compared with their white counterparts.[25] The view that violence against women trumps other violence, including abuse by law enforcement officials in communities of color, has been a distinguishing feature of the mainstream feminist movement against domestic abuse since its inception in the 1960s.[26]

Mainstream feminists justify mandatory arrest, prosecution, and reporting policies by claiming that extraordinary measures are necessary to overcome the sexism that is pervasive in the criminal justice system. What they do not see is that these mandatory policies are also sexist and discriminatory; the policies allow the state to continue to ignore the specific needs and desires of women and men in abusive relationships.

The mainstream feminist paradigm needs to be challenged at its core. I believe that little has changed fundamentally in the last thirty years if mainstream feminists have substituted their own voices for the voices of women like Monique Brown. Mandatory policies put her in a no-win situation that led to the legal system, in effect, re-abusing her. First, Monique Brown's husband did not listen to her, then the police did not listen to her, and finally the prosecutor did not listen to her. The jury heard her out, but only to a limited extent. At no point was Monique Brown offered any attention or support. She was treated like the little girl, Sara, in the story with which this chapter began. Monique Brown was not frightened of fire or a terrorist attack; she was scared of her husband and his violence. The state responded much as Sara's mother initially responded. The police and the legal system said, "We will make the violence go away. Trust us and it will all be okay." But it wasn't true. As the story of Sara illustrates, we do not solve a problem by irrationally believing that we can eradicate violence, plain and simple. As Sara so well understood, we have to move toward the source of our fears if we can have any hope of overcoming them. This involves looking at the violence directly, understanding its complexities, and examining the options for addressing it. Similar to what Sara's mother did when she visited the fire station, the hospital, and the World Trade Center site, we must dialogue with the people who are there for help and create systems that address the violence rather than judge it or look away. We should visit the source of our fears—ground zero—and take the time to understand the causes and dynamics of violence. We must move closer to the source of our fear while beginning the work, finally, of learning to heal the violence.

TWO

Mandatory Policies as Crime

Reduction Strategies

Do They Work?

FOR MANY MAINSTREAM FEMINISTS, POLICIES SUCH AS
mandatory arrest, mandatory prosecution, and mandatory reporting
represent significant progress in forcing the state to take domestic violence crimes seriously. After years of indifference to intimate abuse, police officers, prosecutors, physicians, and judges are now mandated to
respond uniformly to crimes between intimate partners. This approach
eliminates both the professional's discretion and the victim's desires
from the state's decision-making process. In this chapter, I will argue
that such policies are mostly symbolic; they do not achieve the instrumental goal of reducing incidents of domestic violence.

Looking back helps to understand both how we arrived at mandatory policies and what steps are still needed to address violence in the
intimate sphere. The history of domestic violence policy making and
practice illuminates why mainstream feminist activists believed drastic
steps were needed. State courts often condoned violence against women
by their husbands or partners and prevented women in abusive relationships from prosecuting their abusers. Spousal abuse was not legally
prohibited until the end of the nineteenth century. However, not until

the 1960s, when the women's movement made domestic violence a "public" issue, did any services develop to address the plight of women in abusive relationships.[1]

Initially, mainstream feminists focused on providing the woman in an abusive relationship with mental health services and a shelter for safety if she sought refuge. The underlying thrust of these programs was to hide and protect the woman and encourage her to separate from her abusive partner. As these services became established, women's advocates shifted from addressing the battered woman's private concerns to highlighting the public's collusion with the violence through the state's inaction. Police officers, prosecutors, and judges were seen as colluding with the batterer and replicating the violence in the intimate relationship by failing to listen to the woman's complaints.

Police officers were generally more lenient in their treatment of intimate abuse perpetrators when compared with other crimes. Such factors as whether the suspect was at the scene when the police officer arrived, whether a weapon or alcohol was involved, the seriousness of the victim's injury, the presence of a witness, and whether a restraining order had been violated have all been found to affect the extent to which police officers responded to domestic violence calls,[2] as opposed to the woman's desire to have the perpetrator arrested.

This overt hostility toward the desires of victims of domestic violence to have their perpetrators arrested caused survivors and feminist advocates to become frustrated with the legal system. Even though they were initially distrustful of the legal system's capacity to protect women from men's violence, they nevertheless committed to transforming it. The Jim Brown case illustrates the cause of their frustration: it was not until 1999 that he was actually prosecuted for a domestic violence crime, even though three different women had lodged significant allegations of intimate violence against him between 1968 and 1986.[3]

In the 1970s, mainstream feminist activists undertook the important project of reforming institutional responses to domestic violence. In time, they fought for the installation of mandatory procedures to force the front line of the criminal justice and health care systems to take domestic violence seriously.[4] Yet these practices do not listen to the

woman's complaints or take seriously her desires to have the perpetrator arrested *or not*; they leave the woman out of the decision-making
process.

Advocates of mandatory arrest, prosecution, and reporting in domestic violence cases argue that these policies force professionals to
treat crimes against women in the same manner in which they treat
other crimes.[5] Mandatory arrest and prosecution, they argue, require
professionals who are reluctant to respond to intimate abuse crimes to
take the same steps they would take in cases in which the assailant is a
stranger and the victim is male.[6] This response, mainstream feminists
argue, has the additional benefit of eliminating racial discrimination
from the criminal justice system, insofar as it ensures that all perpetrators, regardless of race, are treated similarly.[7]

Supporters of mandatory interventions believe that these approaches keep battered women safer than under the previous system
when no arrest was made or prosecution initiated. Citing a previous
study on the effectiveness of arrest in Minneapolis and the replication
studies that followed, some mainstream feminists have argued that
when police officers intervene—regardless of the battered woman's
wishes—future incidents of violence against women are deterred.[8]

Mainstream feminist advocates also believe that these proactive
policies structurally alter the politics of gender violence. A strong stand
against intimate abuse, accompanied by legal sanctions, is evidence of
the state's evolving feminist consciousness. At least in theory, police
officers, prosecutors, medical personnel, and judges no longer collude
with batterers by ignoring violence inflicted on women. This approach,
proponents argue, dismantles sexism at the level of institutions and
achieves the overarching goal of decreasing discrimination against
women.[9]

The problem is that the mainstream feminists' goal of reforming
criminal justice practice at the systemic level was overly ambitious. By
changing the actions of police officers, prosecutors, medical personnel,
and judges, they wanted to change the discriminatory attitudes that led
to the collusion with batterers to which they objected. In doing so,
mainstream feminists lost sight of their initial goal of incorporating the
voice of the battered woman into the criminal justice system.[10] Instead,

as I will show, they began replacing individual battered women's desires with their own. As it became clear that the diversity of women's voices had become lost, other feminists became concerned.[11] By closely examining mandatory arrest, prosecution, and reporting policies as they have been practiced and enforced, I aim to give voice to this rising concern.

MANDATORY ARREST

Mandatory or pro-arrest policies require an officer to arrest a suspect if there is probable cause to believe that an assault or battery has occurred, regardless of the victim's consent or objection. This policy, depending on how stringently it is applied, eliminates or hampers police discretion in intimate abuse cases.

Mandatory arrest first became the preferred policy in 1984 when Lawrence Sherman and Richard Berk published their landmark study of the relationship between arrest and recidivism in domestic violence criminal cases. Using a sample size of 314 cases, Sherman and Berk concluded that arrest was the most effective means of preventing batterers from becoming violent again.[12] This study, conducted in Minneapolis, was the first of six randomized field experiments that tested the relationship between police intervention and recidivism or future incidents of violence.[13] On the heels of this study, the U.S. Attorney General recommended that arrest become the standard response to misdemeanor domestic violence cases.[14] In 1986, a survey of U.S. police departments revealed that one-third had changed their arrest policies in domestic violence cases because of the Minneapolis findings.[15]

Other police departments changed their lax policies in intimate abuse cases when civil awards to victims began costing them precious resources. In 1979, the daughter of a batterer was awarded a $2 million judgment in *Sorichetti v. City of New York* after her father attacked her with a fork, a knife, and a screwdriver and attempted to saw off her leg during a visitation. The New York Court of Appeals held that the court order of protection in this case created a special duty on the part of the authorities to protect the battered woman and her daughter. Thus, the Court found the New York City Police Department liable when officers failed to investigate reports that the daughter had not returned from the visit with her father.[16]

Likewise, in 1984, Tracey Thurman was awarded $2.9 million after suing the Police Department of Torrington, Connecticut, and twenty-four city police officers on the grounds that the city's policy and practice of nonintervention and nonarrest in domestic violence cases was unconstitutional. Tracey Thurman's estranged husband was on probation for smashing the windshield of her car while she sat inside. Police failed to arrest him on many occasions, even when he violated both the terms of his probation and a restraining order. On June 10, 1983, Tracey Thurman called the police. By the time an officer arrived she had already been repeatedly stabbed and was severely injured. The court found a violation of the Fourteenth Amendment's equal protection clause because Thurman was able to prove that the police department treated violence by a male friend or relative differently from crimes committed by strangers. The court interpreted this deviation as sex discrimination.[17]

Currently, the federal government encourages state interventions, including mandatory arrest and prosecution, by providing federal funds to jurisdictions that adopt stringent domestic violence policies.[18] Today, every state, except Arkansas and Washington, D.C., has codified its mandatory or pro-arrest policies.[19] Some studies have shown that police officers are becoming increasingly responsive to mandatory arrest provisions in the law. In response, many mainstream feminists now believe that mandatory arrest policies are one of the most effective methods for ensuring that police officers arrest batterers for their crimes.[20]

The problem is that such policies may be less effective than they appear, and strong empirical evidence suggests that mandatory arrest may actually increase the incidence of violence in some women's lives. In 1992, Lawrence Sherman and his colleagues conducted a study in Milwaukee on the effects of arrest on batterers in that city. The study design recognized three possible interventions: full arrest, short arrest, and no arrest (with a warning if police were called back). Sherman found that full or short arrest had a short-term deterrent effect. Over the long term, however, violence increased in cases in which the perpetrator had been arrested. Although there were several indicators of this trend, one of the most telling is the calculation by researchers of the number of days it took for repeat violence to occur during the entire period of the study (twenty-two months). The group of offenders who were randomized into the arrested group and who repeated their violence did so in 124 days. The group of offenders who were randomized into the group that received warnings, and who repeated their violence, did so in 160 days. The researchers concluded that the offenders who were arrested and who repeated their violence did so 23 percent sooner than the group of offenders who were warned.

Another important finding involved who among the arrested suspects tended to repeat their violence. Violence decreased when the persons arrested were employed, married, and Caucasian. This variable examined in isolation suggests the importance of a mandatory arrest policy in deterring future acts of violence. However, when it is combined with other factors, such as who is likely to be arrested by criminal justice personnel, a different picture emerges. Sherman found that when Milwaukee police arrest 10,000 African American men for domestic violence crimes, these arrests produce 1,803 *more* acts of domestic violence primarily against African American women. If these men had been warned and not arrested, according to Sherman's findings, these acts of violence may not have occurred or would have been delayed. When, on the other hand, Milwaukee police arrest 10,000 Caucasian men, they produce 2,504 *fewer* acts of domestic violence against Caucasian women when compared with cases in which the Caucasian men are warned. Without considering who actually gets arrested, it appears that a mandatory arrest policy does in fact prevent more acts of violence than it is likely to cause. However, when one considers who is most likely to get arrested by criminal justice personnel, a very different picture emerges. Sherman surmised that if three times as many African American men as Caucasian men are arrested in Milwaukee (which would be typical, given police practices in that city), a mandatory arrest policy would prevent 2,504 acts of violence primarily against Caucasian women, at the price of 5,409 acts of violence primarily against African American women. Sherman concluded that mandatory arrest policies are highly problematic.[21]

Alisa Smith, in a recent study of battered women, illuminates the racial divide that Lawrence Sherman and his colleagues uncovered. Smith studied battered women's attitudes about mandatory arrest and found differences in levels of support for mandated policies between Caucasian and African American battered women. Seventy-nine percent of Caucasian women supported the adoption of mandatory arrest policies, compared with 53 percent of the African American women surveyed. Although other studies have concluded that African American battered women call the police more often,[22] Smith's finding suggests that they may use police services because they have no other available domestic violence resources in their communities.[23] As law professor Kimberlé Crenshaw has argued, it is critical to remember that many women of color are reluctant to seek intervention from the police, fearing that their contact with law enforcement will exacerbate the system's assaults on their public and private lives.[24]

In another study done in Omaha, the researchers confirmed Sherman's general finding that arrest was no more effective a response than interventions such as separation or mediation.[25] In Charlotte, North Carolina, researchers found that arrest did not deter recidivism any more than either advisement or separation.[26] A Colorado Springs study found that arrest did not deter unemployed batterers, concluding that in Colorado Springs, "an arrest can sometimes make things worse."[27] Finally, a study of Dade County, Florida found similar results with regard to unemployed batterers, namely, that arrest only marginally affected recidivism after six months.[28]

As shown earlier, cumulatively, studies on the preventive effects of mandatory arrest found that the positive deterrent of arrest diminished over time. An investigation of combined data found that an arrest deterred "good-risk" perpetrators, who were more likely to suffer embarrassment and stigmatization from the arrest, but did not deter "bad-risk" offenders, whose violence might escalate as a result of the arrest.[29] A good-risk perpetrator was defined by the offender's ties to the community, such as whether the person was employed or married—in other words, whether the person had a lot to lose from the arrest.[30]

Overall, the arrest studies have suggested a need to individualize intervention strategies rather than creating a one-size-fits-all approach. Ideas for reform have focused mostly on modifying the system's response to domestic violence while continuing to recognize the overall utility of criminal justice interventions. For example, Lawrence Sherman and his colleagues have suggested replacing mandatory arrest with mandatory action, or action chosen from a list of possibilities that include providing the victim with transportation to a shelter and the offender transportation to a detoxification center, granting the victim the option to decide if an arrest should be made, and giving suggestions for victim protection.[31] Sherman also suggests that "victim-directed" arrest would allow the person who is more directly affected by the decision to determine whether or not an arrest is beneficial.[32] Taken together, these arrest studies suggest the need to reevaluate what role the woman should play in defining how the system should respond.

MANDATORY PROSECUTION

Following on the heels of mandatory arrest, and as a natural extension of it, prosecutors, through pressure from mainstream feminists, began to develop policies known as mandatory or no-drop prosecution. Some no-drop policies encourage prosecutors to pursue domestic violence cases regardless of the battered woman's wishes.[33] Other no-drop policies are more flexible, involving the possibility of integrating the battered woman's desires into the prosecution process.[34] To address the problem of battered women's reluctance to testify against their batterers, some prosecutors have begun to treat these cases as though no victim was available to testify. Prosecutors try these cases in the same manner in which they conduct murder trials—without the primary witness, namely, the victim.[35] Spontaneous statements made by the victim at the time of arrest, videos or photographs taken at the time of injury, and police officers' evidence form the case against the batterer, rather than the victim's live testimony.

In one national study published in 1996, two-thirds of prosecutors' offices had adopted no-drop policies.[36] Although the presence of these policies suggests that domestic violence cases are all pursued equally, studies of the practices of prosecutors reveal significant variation in how these policies are applied. In one study, the larger the city, the less likely the victim's cooperation would affect the decision to prosecute.[37] Smaller jurisdictions will need the woman's testimony because they have limited resources to gather corroborative evidence from neighbors or family members.[38] The significance of the victim's injuries can also strengthen a case involving a woman who refuses to testify. For example, the New York City Police Department has begun to chronicle domestic violence cases with digital photographs—thus capturing the "clear and detailed images of injuries like swollen eyes, bruised cheeks and handprints around the neck" for future use in trials in which the victims themselves may not cooperate.[39] In the end, given that most victims of domestic violence are reluctant to testify, a case's outcome is determined by the degree to which the prosecutor's office is willing to encourage or force the woman to testify.

Very few studies have tested the effectiveness of mandatory prosecution policies in eliminating or reducing violence against women in abusive relationships. The one randomized study specific to the topic suggested mixed results at best. Ford and Regoli analyzed prosecution policies in Indianapolis, comparing mandatory prosecution and drop-permitted policies in misdemeanor domestic violence cases. In their study of 480 men charged with misdemeanor assault of a conjugal partner, the researchers randomly assigned the batterer to one of three tracks: (1) pretrial diversion to a counseling program, (2) prosecution to conviction with a recommendation of counseling as a condition of probation, or (3) prosecution to conviction with presumptive sentencing. Ford and Regoli found that when victims had initiated the warrant, filed charges under a drop-permitted policy and then chose to prosecute, they were at lower risk for re-abuse following adjudication of the case. In sharp contrast, victims under a drop-permitted policy who chose not to prosecute after having already initiated proceedings had the greatest risk of re-abuse—even greater than for those who were placed in the no-drop prosecution category.

Ford and Regoli pondered why the victim who decided to proceed with a case in a drop-permitted jurisdiction was least likely to experience repeat violence. They concluded that this victim, the one who *chose* to prosecute, derived a kind of personal power from this decision. This power, Ford and Regoli surmised, is derived from three sources: (1) providing women with the possibility of prosecution as a bargaining chip, (2) providing women a means of allying with others (including police, prosecutors, and judges), and (3) providing women a voice in determining sanctions for the batterer.[40] This conclusion underscores the significance of enhancing victim power when the system intervenes rather than undermining it. This point about a victim's personal power has been confirmed in other studies as well.

In 1984, Sherman and Berk tested the effectiveness of arrest in reducing subsequent incidents of violence. In the course of this study, they noticed a difference in recidivism rates when victims perceived police concern as compared with recidivism rates when victims did not perceive police concern. They found that when batterers were arrested and victims did not perceive that the police were concerned and willing to listen, victims were likely to experience repeat abuse in 26 percent of cases. But when batterers were arrested and victims perceived that the police were concerned and willing to listen, the rate of recidivism decreased to 9 percent. Sherman and Berk hypothesized, like Ford and Regoli, that the recidivism rate decreased when victims perceived police interest because the victim felt empowered by the interaction.[41]

To further test Sherman and Berk's findings and to understand victims' satisfaction with how police responded to victims when they arrived at the scene, Buzawa and colleagues studied factors associated with police officers' decisions to arrest the perpetrator when the decision to arrest was not mandated. Such factors as the presence of bystanders or the offender, evidence of a weapon, the living situation of the victim and offender, the seriousness of the victim's injuries, and the victim's preference affected the officer's decisions. Police arrested batterers in 44 percent of the cases in which the victims expressed a desire to prosecute and in 21 percent of the cases in which the victim opposed the arrest. They found that victim satisfaction with police response was almost entirely dependent on whether the officers followed the victim's wishes. Accordingly, a victim expressed increased satisfaction if the police officer followed her request, whether or not the arrest of the perpetrator was warranted. Although Buzawa et al. did not test the links between satisfaction and empowerment or between satisfaction and recidivism, they did confirm the important principle that victims felt comforted when the police followed their wishes.[42] The findings of all these studies underscore the importance of how professionals such as police officers relate to the victim, a topic I address more fully in the next chapter.

More recent studies of mandatory prosecution policies only serve to confirm that the effectiveness of such policies in reducing subsequent incidents of violence is questionable. For example, after Davis, Smith, and Nickles reviewed a large sample (1,133 cases) of domestic violence misdemeanors, they found that prosecution had no effect on the likelihood of rearrest of the batterer within a six-month period. More specifically, Davis and his coauthors determined that recidivism was unaffected by whether a case was dropped, dismissed, or prosecuted. The authors warned that their findings were tentative, but they nevertheless "found no evidence that prosecution outcomes affected the likelihood of recidivism in domestic violence misdemeanor cases."[43] Similarly, McFarlane, Willson, Lemmey, and Malecha found in a smaller study (involving ninety abused women who were interviewed at three and six months after their abusive events) that "whether the women had sufficient evidence for charges to be written by the police or accepted by the district attorney, as well as whether the suspect was arrested or remained a fugitive, made no difference in the amount of violence she reported at the time of filing charges or 3 and 6 months later."[44]

Each of these findings regarding mandated prosecution suggests its equivocal effect on reducing violence against women. These findings beg the question raised in the next chapter: Why have mainstream feminists pursued these policies so vehemently?

MANDATORY REPORTING BY MEDICAL PERSONNEL

Most doctors, nurses, and social workers already follow mandatory reporting rules for injuries that do not necessarily come from intimate abuse. Since 1998, forty-one states have had statutes that require health care practitioners to report injuries that appear to be caused by a knife, firearm, or other deadly weapon. Twenty states and Washington, D.C., require reports when the practitioner believes that the injuries are the result of a criminal or illegal act or otherwise related to the commission of a crime or offense of violence. Eight states require reports of injuries that practitioners believe are the result of an act of violence, which in some cases must be in connection with a criminal act. Six states specifically require reports under circumstances in which the injury appears to be inflicted intentionally or was otherwise not accidental. In nine states, the seriousness or gravity of the injury is important to the health practitioner's decision to report. As of 1998, five states had mandatory reporting laws that specifically required health professionals to call the police or other designated governmental agency when domestic violence or adult abuse, including spousal rape, is suspected.[45]

Women in violent relationships, however, are conflicted about mandatory reporting policies. Coulter and Chez found that battered women support mandatory reporting "for others." When asked to imagine how mandatory reporting would have affected their own abusive situations, female respondents were reluctant to acknowledge its relevance. Half the women interviewed said they would not visit physicians who were mandated to report incidents of domestic violence.[46] Alisa Smith observes a similar phenomenon in her study. A majority of the women supported adoption of mandatory reporting policies, yet when the same women were asked if such policies would benefit them, fewer answered in the affirmative. "Of greater concern," Smith further observes, "is the relatively large percentage of victims reporting that mandatory laws would actually reduce their chance of reporting future incidents of domestic violence."[47]

This is not to say that medical professionals have no role in helping women in abusive relationships. On the contrary, medical professionals can be extremely influential. As the following studies suggest, doctors are the professionals who have the most contact with women in abusive relationships. In a 1991 survey, the American Medical Association asked survivors of domestic violence to identify one person who could have had an impact in preventing their injuries. Eighty-seven percent named their family physician.[48] As reported by Stark and Flitcraft, one in five battered women had seen a physician at least eleven times for trauma. Similarly, Stark and Flitcraft found that 23 percent of battered women had presented six to ten injuries resulting from abuse. Moreover, many visits by women in abusive relationships involve general complaints that are not directly indicative of trauma, including visits in which they seek treatment for anxiety, depression, and other vague medical complaints.[49]

Psychiatric problems also bring victims of domestic violence into contact with medical professionals. Carmen and colleagues found that half of the women they surveyed who had sought psychiatric treatment had physical and/or sexual abuse histories—and 90 percent of those incidents involved family members.[50] Suicide attempts are also common markers for domestic violence: about 25 percent of women who attempt suicide are victims of intimate abuse.[51] Straus and Smith found that depression and suicide attempts are four times more likely in female victims of severe assault than in women who were not subjected to violence.[52] Similarly, alcohol and drug addiction may also provide evidence that a woman is in an abusive relationship. A study by Barnett and Fagan revealed that the incidence of alcohol use by women during an abusive episode was 17.8 percent, whereas the incidence of alcohol use for men was 30 percent. Following the abuse, 48.1 percent of women drank, compared with 24.2 percent of the men.[53]

In studies reported by Stark and Flitcraft, the researchers found that 19 percent of women presenting at emergency rooms were there because of symptoms related to ongoing abuse.[54] In a study of emergency department visits in 1994, the Department of Justice found that 37 percent of injuries to women involved a spouse, ex-spouse, or boyfriend.[55]

But although doctors attend to women in abusive relationships, they do not necessarily uncover abuse. In a 1993 survey conducted by the Commonwealth Fund's Commission on Women's Health at Columbia University, 92 percent of women who were physically abused by their partners did not discuss these incidents with their physicians.[56] In a study of the effect of mandatory domestic violence reporting on health care practitioners in California, Laura Lund found that law enforcement agencies received "relatively few" reports of domestic violence

from health practitioners—and nearly all of these reports were generated by hospital emergency rooms.[57]

McFarlane, Parker, and Soeken found that abuse during pregnancy
affects one in every six adult women and one in five teenagers.[58] Yet
when the Department of Obstetrics and Gynecology at the Maricopa
Medical Center surveyed all obstetrics and gynecology residencies in
the United States and Puerto Rico, it found that 75 percent of medical residents reported that they did not recognize any situations of
battering when presented with "common clinical scenarios of battered women."[59]

Sugg and Inui's 1992 study suggests that doctors' behaviors are
partly to blame. To measure doctors' reluctance to address domestic
violence in their practices, Sugg and Inui interviewed thirty-eight
physicians in a large, urban health maintenance organization serving
predominantly Caucasian, middle-class patients. When asked why
they did not intervene in suspected domestic violence situations, the
physicians cited lack of time and resources, coupled with a hesitation
to interfere in private "family matters." One physician's sentiments
seemed to reflect the group's collective response: he did not want to
"open Pandora's box."[60]

Because women in abusive relationships often have myriad medical
needs, they could benefit if doctors became more attuned to intimate
abuse in ways that empowered women rather than deterred them from
seeking help. Because mandatory reporting is the most recent addition
to the arsenal of mandatory interventions, the verdict is still out on its
effectiveness in preventing future incidents of violence. Given that
women in abusive relationships are likely to visit a health care facility,
supporters of mandatory reporting laws hold out hope that this policy
will ensure arrest and prosecution of a batterer at the earliest possible
point. Others believe that these policies have not adequately incorporated women's concerns that mandatory reporting may, in the abstract,
be a good idea, but may not be especially responsive to their needs.[61]
Whether it is health care, arrest, or prosecution, we need to design systems that welcome women's complex reactions to abuse and seek to increase rather than undermine their personal power in order to prevent
subsequent incidents of violence.

ASSUMPTIONS EMBEDDED IN
MANDATORY POLICIES

Mainstream feminists have consistently asserted the efficacy of mandatory arrest and prosecution policies despite the mounting evidence that they are less effective than was initially assumed. In addition, several feminist advocates assert their support for mandatory reporting policies despite their potentially harmful effect on women who might be deterred from seeking health care for their injuries or for manifestations of the abuse, including depression or addiction. But a growing group of dissenters, myself included, believe that support for these policies is founded on several faulty assumptions, such as those exposed in chapter 1, that remain hidden from public view and are worth exposing.[62]

One assumption not yet discussed is that the state has a responsibility to protect its citizenry, even when mandatory policies may have a negative effect on the people the state aims to protect.[63] In fact, feminist advocates often justify their decision to disregard a woman's desire not to press charges on the grounds of protecting women by assuming they are too weak to protect themselves. As San Diego's city attorney, Casey Gwinn, and police sergeant Anne O'Dell have argued, the only way to overcome women's weakness and the batterer's power is "to take the responsibility out of the hands of the victim and place it with the State where it belongs."[64]

But if the state simply worries about protecting women, it fails them. A woman who appears to be temporarily protected from an abusive partner through his arrest may experience more rather than less violence as a result of that arrest. In addition, a woman needs more than just protection against violence. She still needs to heal and recover, within or outside of her relationship. Yael Danieli, a psychoanalyst who worked extensively with Holocaust survivors, suggests that society's collective responsibility to survivors of trauma is to "share its members' pain. . . . When [members of society] fail to listen and understand, they participate in the *conspiracy of silence* and may inflict further trauma on the survivor or 'the second injury to victims.'"[65] We must focus not only on protecting women, as the next several chapters argue, but also on interrupting patterns of violence and eradicating the underlying dynamics that cause these ruptures in the first place.

A related assumption of mandatory interventions is that battered women are not only too weak to protect themselves but also too fragile, mentally ill, unruly, or indecisive to be able to protect themselves or to participate in their healing. Some law enforcement officials believe that survivors suffer from a syndrome that prevents them from knowing what they *really* want. These police officers and prosecutors think that the battered woman really wants to see the batterer punished, but that she is too easily influenced or otherwise too mentally ill to say, and in response, mandated policies are what she *really* wants, but cannot ask for. Assistant U.S. Attorney Robert Spagnoletti, chief of the Domestic Violence Unit for the District of Columbia, found a related problem. He interviewed "tens of thousands of victims," and "the one thing that became apparent to [him] after a year of this is that [he could not] tell a thing [about what the victim really wants]."[66] Because *he* could not tell which victims were intimidated and which victims made "an informed, voluntary and knowing" decision not to pursue prosecution, he concluded that a no-drop policy that did not "make any differentiation between domestic violence as a crime and any other crime" made the most sense.[67] Another excuse given for these policies, often muttered only in whispers, is that victims are just "too difficult." Spagnoletti's comment that "there is no way to tell" what victims want expresses this frustration. Donald Rebovich's 1996 study of large prosecutorial offices reports that one-third of prosecutors surveyed believe that over 55 percent of female victims are "uncooperative."[68]

When professionals react this way, they may simply be expressing countertransference reactions: their unconscious need to silence or mask their own feelings of guilt, rage, and shame associated with violence in their own personal or even professional lives. As I will explore in chapters 3 and 4, these unexpressed feelings are not without consequences; they infect the professional's relationship with women and men in abusive relationships and reduce the possibility of developing a healing approach that has real potential for human transformation.

It is understandable that professionals are likely to feel overwhelmed by women's abuse histories, helpless in the face of women's desires to remain with partners who are abusive, and frustrated when survivors of intimate abuse do not react in ways that appear to be self-protective. Women's stories of abuse are painful to hear. For professionals who are not trained to anticipate how their own reactions are likely to be transferred onto the clients they are assigned, women's abuse histories can be threatening and sometimes unbearable. Instead of working through their own feelings in ways that promote healing interventions with women in violent relationships, some professionals may become infected by the violence they witness and inadvertently reproduce some of its most destructive forms.[69]

If not interrupted, these unconscious reactions can lead professionals to feel grandiose, even almighty. One commentator, working in a psychiatric setting with trauma victims, has described this phenomenon: "To usurp such a Godlike role is not only outside the authorized function of the psychiatric expert, but, in fact, is an acting out . . . which will be detrimental to the doctor's function and health. Yet, the impulse to play God [in trauma cases] is as ubiquitous as it is pathogenic."[70]

Mandatory intervention policies assume this omnipotence. The policies assume that the state can act as the woman's "omnipotent savior" by taking the decision of how to proceed in her abusive relationship out of her hands. Unconscious of their "impulse to play God," professionals such as police officers and prosecutors, and the mainstream feminists who promote these policies, arrogate the woman's decision making. Paradoxically, as we have seen, mandating a response may rob a woman of the most important resource she has to counteract the violence: her personal power. A critical and related issue is the kind of power mainstream feminists and professionals assert over women in abusive relationships. This topic is developed in the next chapter.

— THREE

Power over Women in Abusive Relationships

MAINSTREAM FEMINISTS EXERT POWER BY DEFINING WHO
women in abusive relationships are and therefore what they should do
about the violence in their lives. Mandatory policies turn professionals
away from women in abusive relationships by focusing so exclusively
on arrest and prosecution and ignoring the opportunity, through human contact, to nurture a relationship with the victim. As we have
seen, this lost opportunity can affect the violence itself. The overall
importance of empowering women in abusive relationships in terms of
safety, and initiating ongoing contact to provide emotional support and
healing, begs the question: Why do mainstream feminists and professionals who carry out mandatory policies so strongly feel the need to
override the desires of women in abusive relationships? I begin to answer this question with the psychoanalytic concepts of transference
and countertransference. I look at the dynamic between women in
abusive relationships and mainstream feminists or helping professionals through a psychoanalytic lens because psychology has been one of
the fields of study to recognize that emotional histories affect all human
interaction. This recognition has been missing from domestic violence
policy and practice, yet clearly the emotional histories of both the feminist and the professional affect the ways they interact with women in
abusive relationships and the way they formulate policy. A therapeutic

relationship therefore has much to teach us about what goes on between people who seek help and people who offer it.

TRANSFERENCE AND COUNTERTRANSFERENCE

In an interaction between a woman in an abusive relationship and a feminist or helping professional, countertransference is the emotional reaction by the professional to the woman's history of abuse. That reaction is informed by the professional's own history of violence. To understand countertransference, we must begin with a discussion of transference.

Transference operates in all therapeutic relationships, including, as I have suggested, between the professional and the woman in the abusive relationship. It is the process by which a client engages with a therapist unconsciously or at a subtextual level to reproduce and work through the abusive events in her past. These ideas are best illustrated through an example.

A woman (I will call her Janet) who was emotionally abused as a child might seek the help of a therapist. In order for that healing work to be deep and meaningful, Janet would have to develop positive and negative feelings toward the therapist that she "transferred" from her own experience of the abuse. Let us assume Janet was emotionally abused by her father, who was very judgmental and disdainful of her, or at least that is how Janet perceived it. If Janet, at some point in the therapeutic relationship, perceived the therapist to be judgmental or disdainful in any small or large way, she would predictably and unconsciously transfer her negative feelings for her father onto her therapist. Janet could then use the therapeutic relationship to better understand her anger toward her father by experiencing some of the same "old" negative feelings in an environment where she could analyze them in the presence of a professional. The safety and security of the therapeutic relationship offer a unique opportunity to examine this history and these residual feelings about the abusive relationship. Janet might even be able to work those feelings through to the point of forgiveness. At a minimum, the therapy would help Janet become aware of her reaction to her father and to people that remind her of her father, her feelings toward them, and how those feelings may interfere in her relationships with others.

One example of Janet's difficulty may be that she experiences most men as judgmental and disdainful, given her history with her father. Janet might seek help from a therapist to understand why she has not been able to sustain a long-term intimate relationship. In the therapy, Janet could learn to recognize her negative reactions to men as they are occurring and better assess whether the men she encounters are truly judgmental and disdainful or only appear to be so because her relationship with her father has so significantly colored how Janet views all men. As the therapist takes on the judgmental and disdainful qualities that Janet "projects" onto him or her (insofar as she projects these qualities onto many, if not most, people), Janet can react to the therapist as she reacts typically when she experiences those feelings. With the therapist's help, Janet sees more clearly how she reacts unconsciously and carries the history of abuse with her to each interaction. When this therapeutic work occurs, Janet begins to understand how and even perhaps why her father treated her as he did.

Forgiveness is not imposed by the therapy but is a natural outgrowth of it as Janet seeks further insight into how the abuse occurred and develops methods for purging herself of the negative feelings she came to embody as a result of it. When Janet learns that her father's judgment and disdain of her were passed on to him through his relationship with one of his own parents, she becomes more sympathetic toward her father. Janet might also realize how cultural, racial, or religious persecution has influenced how her father reacted to her. When Janet comes to understand how much of her father's judgment and disdain she, too, embodies, as well as her own relationship to her cultural, racial, or religious identities, she often softens her anger toward her father and toward herself. At this point of insight, true healing begins to be possible. The rest of the therapeutic work, which is often a lifetime's effort, becomes an ongoing process of discovering other hidden manifestations of how Janet's history with her father gets expressed in Janet's other relationships.

In addition to the anger I have described, clients such as Janet, especially those who are victims of severe physical or emotional violence, are also likely to experience other feelings toward professionals with whom they develop a transference relationship. For example, on the one hand, if Janet had experienced severe abuse, she may not expect the professional to respond to her feelings of fear and helplessness, given how abandoned she felt while the abuse was occurring. On the other hand, she may also unconsciously expect to be rescued by the professional, who she hopes will become her "omnipotent" savior. Janet might even develop the expectation that the professional can protect her from the feelings associated with the severe abuse she experienced, or even from the abuse itself.

Even a therapist who helps Janet feel protected can inevitably disappoint her. Given the delicacy of this emotional work and the imperfections of humans, the therapeutic relationship is fallible, too, and especially so when it involves people who have experienced severe abuse and who seek help to treat it. Because of the sensitivities involved with abuse—the human violation that is involved—the process is subject to many problems. For example, the therapist may fail to elicit sufficient detail of the abuse through questioning, leaving a client feeling as if the therapist does not really care what happened. Similarly, the therapist might overlook feelings associated with a client's emotional need to discuss the abuse, causing the client to remain closed off to her emotional reactions to the abuse. Alternatively, the therapist may listen too closely to the details about the abuse, and the client may interpret this response as voyeuristic.[1]

Significantly abused clients can often read the therapist's every move. According to Judith Herman, "chronically traumatized patients have an exquisite attunement to unconscious and nonverbal communication."[2] Emanuel Tanay, who has worked extensively with survivors of the Holocaust, reports that the therapist must be very careful to avoid blocking the patients' "process of expression and catharsis" because "one question or even a glance which is 'out of tune' and the 'psychological closing off' is re-established."[3]

Given how transference operates, it is critical that helping professionals and other people who encounter women in abusive relationships be flexible enough to respond to these complicated and uniquely individualized sentiments and reactions. For example, some women in abusive relationships are likely to prefer working with a professional who can listen without interrupting them; other women will want the professional to ask detailed questions that enable them to tell their stories. Police officers, prosecutors, physicians, and judges should be attuned to these diverse needs and should be trained to expect a complex set of reactions that vary depending on the person and the abuse. They must also be trained to be aware of their own reactions, what therapists call "countertransference."

Countertransference is as important to the client-therapist relationship as the transference just described. Countertransference is the therapist's reaction to the emotional reaction presented by the client. Often evoked by the client's transference experience, countertransference is therefore also likely to involve an unconscious response. Taking the example described earlier of Janet and her father, it is important to remember that the therapist (I will call her Leona) is also battling her own demons (although presumably the therapist is further on in her healing process and therefore at least more aware of them). If Leona, too, experienced judgment and disdain in her own parental relationship, she might react positively or negatively to Janet once Janet's transference reaction is in full swing. Because this work occurs at the unconscious level, it may take some time before Leona realizes what is happening. During that unconscious period, she may, as described earlier, not respond to Janet in ways that facilitate Janet's comfort. If Leona, for example, does not elicit sufficient detail from Janet about the abusive relationship, Janet may withdraw; if Leona elicits too much detail, Janet might become angry. Assuming Leona is skilled, she will be attuned to these unconscious influences early in the relationship and will recognize what is occurring between her and Janet. Leona, in turn, can adjust, becoming aware of how her own history may be preventing her from being attuned to Janet's precise needs. This therapeutic challenge has been documented by psychoanalysts who have worked extensively with clients who have experienced significant trauma. The countertransference "pull," as it has been called, is so powerful that, as Carl Jung suggests, the psychoanalyst is as much "in the analysis" as the patient.[4] When thought of together, transference and countertransference are what provides the most hope for working problems through at the deepest emotional level.

Yael Danieli is a psychoanalyst who has studied both Holocaust-survivor and nonsurvivor therapists who treat Holocaust survivors and their children. The Holocaust experience evokes feelings in clients similar to those reported by clients who have been physically or emotionally abused. Danieli details several countertransference reactions that can disrupt the therapeutic relationship through the therapist's negative reactions to the client. When revealed, these reactions, including "conspiracy of silence," "bystander's guilt," "rage," and "shame," can help make professionals aware that they are responding negatively to their clients' violent histories.[5]

According to Danieli, a "conspiracy of silence" occurs when the therapist represses discussion of a particular topic or feeling. Danieli proposes that this phenomenon helps the therapist "contain" the difficult feelings the abuse evokes *in the therapist*.[6] This censure can take one of two forms: the therapist may prevent a client from sharing, or the therapist may direct how the client's story should be revealed. Psychoanalyst Henry Krystal has also observed this phenomenon. He finds that therapists who work with Holocaust survivors commonly conduct the therapeutic interview "in a 'questionnaire' fashion": "[I]n some cases, auxiliary personnel in the form of 'history takers' were utilized by examiners. Thus, the expert made contact with a report rather than with a living person."[7]

"Bystander's guilt," another reaction by therapists to a client's history of violence, usually manifests itself in the therapist's feeling that she leads a happy and protected life, especially compared with the client's life of suffering.[8] Bystander's guilt may also arise when the therapist's own history of abuse is evoked by a client's story and the therapist finds her own experience of violence inadequate in comparison. Bystander guilt can have negative consequences in the therapist-client dynamic. For example, the therapist's guilt may manifest in the form of protection toward the survivor (and her children). The therapist may believe that he or she has a responsibility to protect the client from further harm. Rather than nurturing the client's own capacity to work through the abusive history, the therapist attempts to protect her from pain. According to Danieli, "such therapists [tend] to do too much for survivors (and their children) to the point of patronizing them and not respecting their strengths."[9]

Another reaction Danieli identifies in therapists working with Holocaust survivors is rage: "They often [report] that they became enraged listening to Holocaust stories and [are] overwhelmed by the intensity of their own reactions."[10] This rage manifests itself in several responses by therapists to their clients. Some therapists blame the victims for "bringing the Holocaust upon themselves."[11] Other therapists repress their feelings of rage out of a fear of revictimizing their already traumatized patients. In either case, both conscious and unconscious rage figures prominently in therapists' feelings toward their patients and will affect the treatment.[12]

Shame is another important response among therapists treating traumatized clients, especially if the therapists themselves are survivors of violence. Danieli describes the way in which many therapists who survived the Holocaust feel ashamed by their own inaction and, in turn, may blame their clients for not fighting back or resisting Nazi violence. They may condemn their clients for being "victims and, as such, weak, vulnerable, and abused."[13] In a similar vein, survivor therapists, depending on how they characterize their own experiences of the Holocaust, might essentialize their clients as either victims or heroes. When viewed as victims, survivors are "passive and helpless," and therapists become "annoyed and impatient and [feel] the need to liberate" these victims.[14] Heroes, on the other hand, are idealized for their bravery. As might be expected, "most therapists generally prefer . . . working with heroes to working with victims."[15] This preference unconsciously reinforces the client's self-blame and perpetuates his or her feelings of helplessness.

Even so, Danieli finds that therapists who did not themselves survive the Holocaust are more judgmental and less empathetic in treating survivors than are survivor therapists. The nonsurvivor therapists express "attitudes, feelings, and myths disparaging to the survivors . . . while viewing the survivors' offspring as the fragile victims."[16] This shift in focus away from the survivor and toward the survivor's children can lead the therapist to unconsciously blame the survivor for her children's suffering.[17]

Danieli's findings and the larger discussion of transference and countertransference are relevant to our inquiry into why some feminists have advocated for mandatory policies that disregard the desires of women in violent relationships and why professionals who work with these women are so attracted to an approach that minimizes or rejects the survivor's point of view. I contend that the negative countertransference reactions described by Danieli mirror the subconscious reactions of mainstream feminists to men and women in abusive relationships. Conspiring to silence women (and men) who have experienced violence, feeling guilty that one's own violence does not rise to the significance of other women's violence, and stereotyping are all natural and predictable reactions, as we saw from Danieli's observations. The countertransference reactions of mainstream feminists and some helping professionals cause them to express rage against the man, shame for the woman, and denial that a woman's complex and individualized story is relevant. These reactions are manifested most clearly in the theories promoted by mainstream feminists to explain why women stay in abusive relationships.

WHY MAINSTREAM FEMINISTS BELIEVE WOMEN STAY: LEARNED HELPLESSNESS AND TRAUMA THEORY

Mainstream feminists argue that women stay in abusive relationships because they are victims; they fear the repercussions of retaliation, or they fear the power and control their batterers exert over them.[18] For the most part, mainstream feminists believe that women in abusive relationships suffer from a helplessness they have learned as a coping mechanism. This theory was first advanced by Lenore Walker to explain why women stay with abusers. In her research Walker found that intermittent abuse of the kind some women are exposed to increases the victim's anxiety and depression and decreases her capacity to make decisions that best suit her needs. Battered women are especially hampered from making the decision to leave abusive relationships. They "learn" in the face of the violence to become "helpless."[19] This theory presupposes women's weakness when confronted with men's violence and their incapacity to overcome it.

Walker's research revealed that a majority of battered women experienced a similar "cycle of violence" despite their distinct relationships. The cycle, which includes phases such as "tension-building," "acute battering incident," and a "honeymoon," provides the key, according to Walker, to why battered women return to their abusive relationships. Each honeymoon phase brings the hope and promise that the outcome of the abuse will be different this time around.[20]

Although aspects of Walker's theory of learned helplessness have been challenged by some feminists, for the most part its tenets still inform the mainstream feminist response to domestic violence: abuse causes women to return to their relationships. When extricated from the abuse through mandatory policies employed by professionals who believe in them, a woman will be forced to see her partner's evil ways. Clearly, this theory ignores the cultural, economic, and emotional reasons why women stay in abusive relationships and assumes that the experiences of some women—the most abused—are the experiences of all women in abusive relationships all the time.

Judith Herman was one of the first trauma experts to think about how trauma theory might be applied to women in abusive relationships. Trauma theory incorporates some aspects of learned helplessness and rejects others.[21] Herman, a psychiatrist, studied the parallels between war veterans, political prisoners, and battered women. Trauma theory moves beyond some of the limitations of learned helplessness by arguing that there is no one predictable response to violence. So while some women leave abusive relationships, others return to their abusive partners in the face of an ongoing threat of violence.[22] In this way trauma theory helps us understand the complex experiences of women in abusive relationships and the variety of decisions they make in relation to violence. But trauma theory still reflects many of the judgments of mainstream feminists in that women in abusive relationships are still considered mentally ill, they are suffering from post-traumatic stress disorder (sometimes referred to as complex post-traumatic stress disorder),[23] a psychiatric condition that carries with it the stigma associated with mental illness, especially the notion that women in abusive relationships are indecisive, weak, and under the influence of another.

Donald Dutton draws on trauma theory to explain why victims are so easily influenced by their abusers. "Traumatic bonding" is "the development of strong emotional ties between two persons, with one person intermittently harassing, beating, threatening, abusing or intimidating the other."[24] Such reactions have been detected in hostages, abused children, members of cults, and battered women. According to Dutton, two key characteristics create the conditions under which victims bond to their abusers: "periodicity of abuse" and "power imbalance." When the violence is periodic, it is interspersed with periods of normal, even positive, behavior. As such, the abused person is prevented from predicting the next attack. When there is a power imbalance, victims come to identify with their oppressors, and often internalize the negative self-images projected onto them.[25] Traumatic bonding, like learned helplessness, suggests that the bonding process occurs as part and parcel of the violence, which means that once the violence occurs, the abuser has a certain influence over the victim that precludes independent decision making.

Trauma theory as it has been applied to intimate abuse has illuminated the complexities of women's reactions to violence and the diversity of responses to be expected from women in abusive relationships. This has been an important step forward in understanding women who stay in abusive relationships. The problem is that trauma theory still promotes a narrow view of women in abusive relationships as helpless and indecisive, insofar as it fails to incorporate other cultural influences on women's attachments to their intimate partners, such as love, religion, race, family, and the deliberate (although sometimes chaotic) decision making they undertake in relation to those cultural influences. In addition, trauma theory does not go far enough to affirm that strength and resilience are part and parcel of the experience of and response to abuse, and that, as such, power can shift between the two partners as they struggle to maintain what little power they have in the face of violence. This issue of power within the couple is discussed in more detail in the next chapter.

Together the theories of learned helplessness and trauma provide explanations for why women stay in abusive relationships that are embedded in stereotypical assumptions about women as weak. These theories have supported mainstream feminist approaches that suggest that battered women's decision making is markedly limited by the abuse and therefore justify mandated policies that limit battered women's decision making. Although these theories may apply to some women or aspects of some women's responses to violence, they in no way tell the whole story.

Because countertransference reactions impede the helper from seeing women as more than just helpless and traumatized victims, the complexities of why women stay in abusive relationships have often been lost. We need to develop a more accurate picture of women in abusive relationships in order to figure out how to help them.

WHY WOMEN STAY

Statistically, women leaving their partners permanently have had approximately five previous separations prior to their ultimate and final dissolution of the relationship. In the end, it is unclear how many women stay in abusive relationships, because the mainstream feminist research has focused so heavily on women who leave.[26] Based on the data we have, we know that women in abusive relationships make many attempts to leave; half may ultimately stay.[27] The leaving and staying reflect not indecision per se but a complex pattern of behavior that involves not only the effect of the violence and the partner's influence but also other psychological and sociocultural factors. Looking at how women act helps us understand those factors more fully.

Whether dictated by genetics or patriarchy, there is overwhelming evidence to suggest, in general, that women tend to have stronger relational bonds than men and, in turn, are more likely to maintain emotional attachments even in the face of danger.[28] Relinquishing an intimate relationship is no easy task. Women agonize over lost lovers and familial relationships gone astray. Many women, as relational beings, are haunted by whether they have tried hard enough. Leaving an intimate relationship triggers sadness about losing the promises offered by love no matter how unfulfilled, as well as fears of being lost without the other.

When violence enters the intimate sphere, it exacerbates the suffering women feel from trying to figure out whether a relationship is worth saving. For some, a slap across the face is just another fight. For others, it is the final straw. A violent intimate relationship is both easier and more difficult to let go. It is easier because the violence provides a concrete reminder that the relationship is dysfunctional. It is more difficult because the memory of the abuse etched into the lovers' minds binds them together in the suffering.[29]

When most women consider leaving an abusive relationship, they do so after understanding the costs.[30] Emotional attachment, love for their children, race, religion, and ethnicity, as well as economic issues, are just a few of the considerations women in abusive relationships must weigh.[31] A woman may feel she must keep the family intact, especially given cultural imperatives that value family over all else. Current U.S. culture places such a strong emphasis on family cohesion that many women feel compelled to weigh these demands over their own safety. In addition, a woman's sympathy or understanding of her partner's abuse, its origins, and even its manifestations can affect how she thinks about staying or leaving. She has very likely witnessed firsthand the judgments her partner feels from his family of origin, or his sense of abandonment by them. Any woman with no education, no job history, and few skills is likely to choose a few violent incidents even if she has a middle-class or upper-middle-class lifestyle.[32]

Women from minority religious and racial communities face unique considerations when deciding whether to leave a violent partner. Leti Volpp observes that to isolate women's experiences as women above religious or racial influences divorces them from the complicated identities that make up their lives. Women cannot live only as women, Volpp argues, because they are part of numerous communities that include racial and religious affinities.[33] Several scholars have described the unique frame of reference within which women of color understand intimate violence, a frame that spans the clinical, political, and legal spectrums. These women face additional pressures to paint a favorable picture of their families and to protect against reinforcing cultural stereotypes that depict minority communities as more violent than the mainstream group. This need to hide the violence is integral to the decisions minority women make with regard to the violence.[34] Some women of color fear that calling the police will subject their partner to brutality; an immigrant woman understands that to prosecute her husband is potentially to jeopardize their family's status in the United States. Most women of color understand the challenges men of color face in relation to such issues as cultural subordination, job insecurity, and the rage and feelings of inadequacy that these experiences foster. Others understand how experiencing abuse as a child can turn a man into a monster. Some women of color feel safe enough to share their experiences of violence with friends, but unsafe when their views are amplified beyond their close-knit communities.[35]

Orthodox Jewish women, on the other hand, may feel afraid to tell anyone in their immediate community of the violence they are enduring for fear that their children may be shunned and judged.[36] Some Muslim women may not want to expose the violence for fear that the reaction will threaten the delicate balance they have created between here and abroad.[37] Religious women in general may feel that it is their moral responsibility to provide a peaceful and hospitable home. Although patriarchy may provide some political insight into these women's unique circumstances, as a method of intervention it only serves to judge them for their choices.

Lesbians experience domestic violence at similar rates as heterosexual women, yet their willingness to divulge the violence in their lives is hampered by the homophobia they are likely to encounter.[38] A mainstream feminist analysis of domestic violence that assumes women are passive or at most defensively violent can lead a lesbian survivor to wonder whether she is exaggerating the violence she is experiencing at the hands of her female lover.

A comprehensive understanding of domestic violence must recognize these contingencies that so often influence women's lives and understandably affect their decision making. Yet mainstream feminists, professionals who adopt mainstream feminist approaches, and the culture at large judge women harshly for staying in the abusive relationship. If only she were not so helpless or traumatized and could have developed a feminist consciousness, mainstream feminist tenets hold, she would realize how terrible her life is and leave. Some feminists have gone so far as to suggest that mandatory arrest and prosecution policies can help women see what is obvious to others, namely, that ending an abusive relationship is their only viable option.[39] This is an expression of the power mainstream feminists or helping professionals exert over women in abusive relationships.

WHY MAINSTREAM FEMINISTS SHOULD BE CRITICAL ABOUT THEIR OWN POWER

Mainstream feminists argue that abusive men do not acknowledge their own power and should be held accountable for it. Yet they, too, are guilty of the same behavior. Taking a closer, more critical look, mainstream feminism often reflects the "white," "middle-class," "heterosexual," and "privileged" interests that assert it.[40] Tensions between Caucasian, middle-class feminists and feminists of color have been highlighted in numerous contexts.[41] Not only are the class and racial backgrounds of mainstream feminists salient to their reactions to domestic violence, but the privilege associated with these and other factors such as their heterosexuality is also relevant. That privilege—to not have to be subjected to the intrusion of the criminal justice system, as people of color are, and to have a platform from which to speak and legislate as powerful white women—has prevented mainstream feminists from developing a method for reflecting on their own power; this has been especially true in the domestic violence context.[42] The racial and class privilege of mainstream feminists may explain, at least in part, why they have failed to consider the importance of cultural, racial, or religious influences on women in violent relationships.

White mainstream feminists have not been interested in how power is asserted but instead have focused almost exclusively on how they think it operates.[43] More specifically, although white middle-class, heterosexual feminists have reflected on the power of patriarchy and its effect on intimate abuse, they have failed to reflect on how their views about patriarchy, learned helplessness, and trauma theory have substituted their own voices for the diversity of women in abusive relationships whose voices need to be heard. This act of substitution itself represents the way mainstream feminists and professionals who adhere to these views maintain power over battered women. Exposing the limitations of a patriarchal analysis of domestic violence and the origins of these views—the unreflected histories of abuse of mainstream feminists and professionals and their countertransference reactions to women in abusive relationships—allows us to see how mainstream feminists use patriarchy to prevent deeper reflection on the genesis of intimate abuse, including their own reactions to it, and especially its dynamic, intergenerational, and intergendered nature.

Mainstream feminists have consistently taken the position that patriarchy is the sole influence on women, and that it dictates how and why they act as they do. This idea that one truth explains all else has often been interpreted simply as the exclusion of women from male culture.[44] If women are excluded in these ways, the argument goes, women have no power. Viewing power as exclusively male allows feminists to ignore their own power and to avoid reflecting on it. Mainstream feminists, in other words, need not see how they assert that power through mandated policies and related practices with women in abusive relationships.

Compare mainstream feminist interpretations of power as one-sided to Michel Foucault's interpretation of power as relational. In the first volume of *The History of Sexuality*, Foucault offers a method for reflecting critically on power in relationships and for analyzing how mainstream feminists have seized power in the domestic violence policymaking arena. Foucault's interest in power concerns not only who has it and who does not but also the way that disempowered people actually wield power. According to Foucault, power never reflects "static forms of distribution"; rather, it involves the constant shifting of power, or "matrices of transformations."[45]

Foucault's interpretation of power as relational and constantly shifting allows for self-reflection in the manner described here. This self-reflective process would enable mainstream feminists to see and understand their power over women in abusive relationships. A self-critical approach that included, first, reflection on their own histories and related countertransference reactions to women in abusive relationships and, second, reflection on their power over explanations for and responses to domestic violence would take us a long way toward rethinking our responses to intimate abuse. Threatening as it may be, mainstream feminists desperately need to undertake this project of self-reflection on their countertransference reactions, to interrupt the abuse they inflict on women in violent relationships through promotion of mandatory practices, and to develop a more productive stance toward the people they want to help. This work would free up mainstream feminists and professionals who adhere to these practices to hear what each woman in an abusive relationship wants and needs, rather than judging all women in an abusive relationship as helpless, dependent, or ill. The freedom to hear what a woman wants and what her needs are frees feminists and professionals to recognize not only helplessness, dependency, and even illness but also the strength, clarity, and deliberate decision making that so often accompany the reactions of a woman in an abusive relationship. This, in turn, contributes to helping each individual woman develop her personal power rather than focusing so exclusively on the lack of power that has come to dominate mainstream feminist thinking.

Some readers might be wondering whether mainstream feminists and professionals really do any damage by asserting these points of view and indeed might feel strongly that the mainstream feminist approach is the only way to alter gender dynamics at a structural level. The relationships between mainstream feminists, professionals, and women in abusive relationships are problematic not only for the emotional reasons described in the discussion on countertransference but also for safety reasons.

As noted earlier, mandatory interventions, by their very nature, rob women in abusive relationships of an important opportunity to take the abuse into their own hands and decide what to do about it. The power dynamics asserted by mainstream feminists and supported by the professionals who apply mandatory policies actually do damage to women who stay in abusive relationships. If women choose to stay in their relationships after having left and encountered mainstream femi-

nist views—a common scenario—they are likely to return to their partners with judgments about themselves as helpless, dependent, or ill.
They return with less clarity, confidence, and, perhaps most important,
personal power than they had before they left. This can be emotionally
and physically damaging.

According to O'Neill and Kerig, battered women who perceive that
they have "control over abuse can moderate the degree of psychological symptoms" in themselves.[46] They also found that women who perceived such control were "resilient in the face of intimate violence."[47]
Herbert, Silver, and Ellard explain the coping strategies women use as
ones in which they "employ cognitive strategies that help them ap-
praise their relationships positively."[48] We also learned earlier that
women who feel this kind of personal power can make decisions that
help keep them physically safer as well.

Rather than seeing women in abusive relationships as mentally ill or
emotionally lacking, a perception that coincides with undermining
women's power, it is useful to construct a new feminist analysis of domestic violence, one that starts with women's perspectives. Re-viewing why
women choose to stay in abusive relationships from a less judgmental
and more self-reflective stance allows us to understand and embrace the
complexities of their decision making and to see these decisions in a new
light. It forces us to question what we assume about women in abusive relationships, and it helps us understand that the professional's goal must
be to see each relationship as uniquely as the couple sees it. If we understand countertransference and mainstream feminism's use of power and
control in the intimate abuse context, we can look more closely at violent relationships. We can look with less fear and anger. To this end, the
next chapter takes up the difficult task of seeing women in violent relationships as aggressive, and coming closer to understanding exactly how
intimate abuse is a dynamic process influenced by both gender and
generation.

FOUR

Are Women as Aggressive as Men?

I FIRST MET BRENDA ARIS AT FRONTERA PRISON IN Southern California, where she was serving a fifteen-year to life sentence for shooting her sleeping husband. Perhaps I expected to meet someone calculating and cruel. Instead, I found Brenda to be kind and docile. Even when I learned her history of abuse, I did not fully understand where she found the strength to kill.

Over the course of many years, Brenda has shared with me the details of that fateful event. Rick Aris, her husband of eleven years, had hit her that night and had threatened her life before he passed out. Brenda did not know when Rick would wake and kill her. She genuinely believed a preemptive strike while he was asleep was her only choice. Most mainstream feminists would agree: Brenda was a victim; her violence was self-defense; and she did not deserve the second-degree murder sentence she received.

While I do not believe that Brenda deserved to serve what was ultimately almost eleven years in prison, I am not sure she was simply a victim. What I do know is that she got the gun from her neighbor's apartment, sat behind her husband on the bed they shared, and shot five bullets toward his back. Rick Aris was a rageful, abusive man. Of that I am certain. I am also certain that Brenda shot that gun, that her violence cannot be denied. This chapter explores the nature of women's violence and asks the critical question, Are women as violent as men? It also helps us understand more clearly how and why women's violence has been given short shrift and how this approach, in turn, has prevented us from addressing the problem more appropriately.

Following the implementation of mandatory interventions, the greatest increase in arrests has been of women who are charged with domestic violence crimes. Los Angeles provides a poignant example: in 1987, a total of 340 women and 4,540 men were arrested for domestic violence crimes in that city. In 1995, after mandatory arrest policies were implemented, 1,262 women and 7,513 men were arrested for domestic violence crimes.[1] Since the implementation of aggressive arrest policies, three times as many women have been arrested for domestic violence crimes, compared with less than twice as many men.

Most mainstream feminists would argue that the problem of dual arrest, as it is sometimes called, lies with a police officer who fails to identify the primary aggressor (the man) and therefore arrests both parties to satisfy the mandate that someone be arrested when a domestic violence crime has occurred.[2] Sexism on the part of police officers, these advocates complain, explains why women have been arrested in such large numbers. To respond to the dual-arrest problem, supporters of mandatory arrest policies have pushed for "primary aggressor" laws that more clearly assign blame to the male perpetrator. Here I ponder a different and more troubling reason for the statistics. What if some part of the reason women are being arrested is because they are involved in a dynamic of intimate abuse?

At the very heart of mandatory policies and the mainstream feminism that supports it lies the assumption that men abuse women and should therefore be punished for their violence. Many mainstream feminists consider it heretical to suggest that women's violence may be a relevant factor in thinking about intimate abuse. They believe that even suggesting that Brenda Aris is in any way responsible minimizes the violence of true batterers, the *real* bad guys like Rick Aris. These mainstream feminists worry that if we question the assumptions upon which domestic violence policy making has been built, we will begin to blame women for men's violence and set the movement back. Yet it is crucial to understand the role of women's violence in the dynamics of intimate abuse if we want to develop new theories and methods that truly address the problem.

WOMEN AS AGGRESSORS

As a preliminary matter, it is helpful to understand more holistically how violence, also referred to as aggression, expresses itself. Björkqvist and Niemela define aggression broadly as "an act done with the intention to harm another person, oneself, or an object."[3] Early work done by Buss and Feshbach and later developed by Björkqvist and Niemelä divides aggression into categories along several continua, including physical versus verbal aggression; instrumental (physical) versus hostile (emotional) aggression; and attack (generally unjustified) versus defense (justified).[4] The pain generated by an aggressive act may be either physical or psychological. As we will see, the term "aggression" encompasses more than just the physicality of violence or abuse that so often defines these terms. A broader definition becomes key when we start to see more clearly how intertwined all forms of aggression can be.

Of course, aggression occurs between individuals, between groups, and even between institutions and an individual or group. The research unequivocally confirms that girls and women are involved in all these forms of aggression. Interpersonal aggression can exist between males and females, males and males, and females and females. Institutionalized aggression, from the death penalty to racial profiling, can be carried out by female state employees just as it can be carried out by male employees. Institutions can also cause discrimination against women through lower wages or through unsafe labor practices. White feminists can discriminate against women of color through such policies as mandatory arrest and prosecution.[5] All of these examples are forms of aggression.

How researchers have defined aggression has obviously shaped the results of their research. For example, researchers in New Zealand found that when they inquired into "aggression" rather than "violence," they were more likely to elicit admissions by women that they were violent. In one study, 37 percent of the women surveyed admitted that they had perpetrated physical aggression against their male partners, compared with 22 percent of men who admitted perpetrating physical aggression against their female partners.[6] Severe physical aggression by women also measured at significant rates. Twenty-four percent of women, versus 8 percent of men, reported using such behaviors as kicking, hitting, biting, hitting with a weapon, slapping, using or threatening the use of a knife or gun, beating up, and choking or strangling.[7] In this same study, 95 percent of the women and 86 percent of the men reported at least one act of verbal aggression against a partner.[8]

When the research question is narrowed to encompass "physical assault" rather than "aggression," the outcome is clearly affected. For example, in a study by Langley, Martin, and Nada-Raja, men were much less likely to identify women's acts of aggression as "assault," whereas women were much more likely to label men's acts of aggression as "assault." Only 2.7 percent of the men and 11.3 percent of the women reported "assaults" by their intimate partners.[9] These findings reflect the results that most mainstream feminists rely on when describing domestic violence: men are abusers, women are victims, and everyone should see it that way.

However, the bulk of studies on abuse in intimate relationships clearly contradict this conclusion. In a startling finding from the United States, Straus, Gelles, and Steinmetz reported in 1974 that husbands and wives committed nearly equal amounts of physical violence in intimate relationships. According to these findings, 12.1 percent of husbands reported that they committed violent acts against their female partners, and 11.6 percent of wives reported acts of violence against male partners. Ten years later, their results were essentially confirmed: 11.3 percent of husbands reported violence against their wives, and 12.1 percent of wives reported violence against their husbands.[10] What is perhaps most interesting about these studies is that they reveal that men and women, in equal numbers, report being the sole victim of violence in the intimate relationship.[11] In other words, these studies do not in any way suggest that women's violence is a reaction to men's violence. More than one hundred studies have since confirmed these and similar findings.[12]

A study of college students affirms that violence between young men and women who are dating and not married is also equal.[13] Other research indicates that high school girls are at least as violent as boys in dating relationships, if not more so.[14]

Violence in lesbian relationships also sheds light on the issue of female aggression. Bowman and Morgan, who studied verbal and physical abuse in homosexual and heterosexual college students, found that in same-sex relationships, lesbians reported statistically significant higher levels of violence in all instances than women in heterosexual relationships.[15] Lockhart and colleagues found that 90 percent of the lesbians they surveyed had experienced verbal aggression over the previous twelve months, and 30 percent reported one or more incidents of physical violence.[16] According to Lie and Gentlewarrier, more than half of the 1,099 lesbians in their study reported that they had been physically abused by a female lover or partner.[17] These statistics suggest that lesbians, and hence women, are not immune from exerting or experiencing violence in their intimate relationships.

Rohner has evaluated the effect of gender and culture on aggression and found that culture predicts or modifies aggression more than gender does.[18] In an effort to learn more about the extent of women's aggression in countries and cultures beyond the United States, Burbank found that women's aggression was evident in all 137 of the societies she studied from around the world.[19] Studies in countries such as Canada, Venezuela, and Mexico also support the finding that women are engaged in aggressive acts toward their partners at least as often as are men.[20]

Even so, gender can, at times, determine the forms that aggression takes. Some researchers have found that traditional gender roles influence how girls and eventually women express their anger and aggression. Passive aggression or "indirect" methods are common expressions of female anger.[21] Because boys and men are often larger and stronger and have higher levels of physical activity, their aggression may be more physical. Girls and women, predictably, draw on their well-developed emotional strength to express aggression.[22]

Björkqvist describes indirect aggression as an attempt to hurt another while avoiding detection.[23] In a study of indirect aggression, Björkqvist found that the purpose of the indirect approach was to "find a strategy as effective as possible, while at the same time exposing the individual to as little danger as possible. Therefore the usefulness of covert, indirect strategies. Verbal strategies, too, put distance to the opponent, and they are accordingly less dangerous than physical aggression. Therefore when verbal skills develop, verbal means of aggression tend to replace physical ones whenever possible."[24]

An example of this kind of indirect aggression occurs when girls use their verbal skills to gossip and backbite or to become friends with someone as a way to hurt others. This kind of indirect aggression increases dramatically around age eleven, especially in girls. Girls form closer friend groups than do boys, and they also develop verbally more quickly. These girls use indirect aggression (sometimes anonymously) to remain part of a clique or a group of close friends.[25] Smith and Thomas found that loneliness, unfair treatment by adults, TV watching, and rejection by classmates all correlated with girls' increased feelings of the desire to hurt someone.[26]

Only a few studies have attempted to identify what other forms of aggression are distinct to females, in addition to the indirect type already described. For example, Kuschel found that Bellonese women sing mocking songs as an effective means of expressing aggression.[27] Burbank found that American women use weapons, destroy property, lock their partners out of the house, and/or refuse to prepare meals or otherwise engage with their partners.[28] Another surprising result was found in a large study of college psychology students, conducted by Muehlenhard and Cook, who reported that 63 percent of male students believed that they had felt peer pressure to engage in "unwanted sexual intercourse" with women. That pressure took the form of peer comments or the desire to be popular. Interestingly, only 46 percent of the female students admitted to engaging in unwanted sexual intercourse.[29]

Another distinct feature of women's aggression is that it is most likely to occur in the context of family. In a large longitudinal study of more than forty-five hundred high school seniors and dropouts in California and Oregon, Ellickson, Saner, and McGuigan found that girls were much more likely to be engaged in hitting family members than they were to be involved in gang violence. Twenty-six percent of both boys and girls reported that they hit or threatened to hit members of their families.[30]

Intimate male partners kill their female partners more often than the reverse. What is striking, however, is how infrequently intimate homicide actually occurs. In 2001 in the United States, 1,034 men killed their female intimate partners, and 295 women killed their male partners.[31] Although men may perform the majority of sexual abuse on women and children in the family, women are more likely to be physically abusive (though the difference between the two groups is not large).[32] As Wauchope and Straus hypothesize, the prevalence of abuse by mothers against their children might reflect their primary caretaking responsibilities. In other words, mothers commit more child abuse because they are more likely to be exposed to a home environment.[33] Interestingly, a report by the Bureau of Justice Statistics found similar rates of murder by mothers and fathers of children under the age of five.[34]

The view that mother's exposure to children explains why women are likely to abuse children does not in any way excuse such behavior. Even verbal abuse by mothers can have devastating consequences for children and later for adults. Psychologist Donald Dutton reports that there may be a critical link between verbal abuse inflicted by the mother on her male child and the likelihood of the boy becoming abusive once he grows up and becomes intimate with a female partner.[35] Dutton's finding that verbal abuse by a mother may cause a man to have extreme anger responses toward his female partner only underscores the importance of recognizing all forms of abuse—physical and emotional, male and female, parent and child—in the violence dynamic.

Mainstream feminist activists and researchers have consistently argued that women's aggression against men is irrelevant because it inflicts so much less harm than the injuries men inflict on women. These scholars argue that psychological or even physical abuse inflicted by women is irrelevant compared with other forms of violence expressed by men.[36] As we will see later in this chapter, this rhetorical and legal strategy of dismissing emotional abuse has the effect of ignoring all women's violence. So if the political imperatives are so great, that is, to expose the injurious nature of men's violence in an attempt to protect women, why do I persist in exposing these less significant forms of women's aggression?

There is strong evidence to suggest that psychological abuse can often predict physical aggression. In a study of engaged and newly married couples, Murphy and O'Leary found that "psychologically coercive behavior precedes and predicts the development of physical aggression in marriage."[37] They also report that both partners "may contribute to the escalation of conflict tactics during the early stages of the relationship."[38] These findings are important for two reasons. They suggest that if feminists' overriding goal is to reduce incidents of violence against women, reducing psychological aggression in both partners is likely to reduce injurious physical abuse against women. They are also important for another less obvious reason. Researchers Kevin Hamberger and Theresa Potente argue that emotional abuse should count less in terms of the hierarchy of violence because it has less potential to oppress.[39] There is evidence that in fact this is not true—some women experience emotional abuse as much more significant than physical forms of violence.[40] If we do not recognize women's emotional aggressiveness, it is difficult to acknowledge the ways men can be emotionally abusive, too.

It is startling, in the face of the studies described here, to realize that mainstream feminists have been so successful at repressing altogether the effect of women's aggression on intimate abuse. The primary rhetorical strategy used by mainstream feminists to achieve this success has been to minimize abuse by women by labeling it as exclusively defensive—a necessary reaction to men's violence.

In fact, when Stets and Straus compared the violence patterns of couples, they found that the most prevalent pattern was one in which women's violence was more severe and men's violence was less significant. Among couples who were dating, 13.5 percent reported that the women had a pattern of more severe violence, and only 4.8 percent reported the male pattern to be more severe. In cohabiting couples, 1.2 percent reported that men's pattern of abuse was more severe, compared with 6.1 percent who reported that women's abuse was more severe. In married couples, 2.4 percent reported a pattern of "more" severe violence for men, compared with 7.1 percent who reported that women represented the more severe pattern.[41]

Let us return to the fact that what is distinct about men's and women's violence is the degree to which women, although aggressive and violent in their own right, are more likely to be injured by men than vice versa. Stets and Straus found that 7.3 percent of the women who reported severe violence against them by men needed medical at-

tention, compared with 1.0 percent of the men reporting severe violence.[42] This is consistent with Berk, Berk, Loseke, and Rauma's study
of 262 domestic disturbance calls. When ranked according to injury, 43
percent of the women were found to have been injured; 7 percent of
male victims had injuries.[43]

Mainstream feminist activists recognized early on the importance of
this distinction to their legal advocacy efforts. Separating emotional
and physical violence meant that female victims of injurious domestic
violence would get legal recognition, and their complaints about the
violence in their intimate lives would be addressed. Indeed, as mainstream feminism developed these judgments about the relative importance of men's violence and the insignificance of women's aggression,
these attitudes became incorporated into the lexicon of the culture at
large. The fact that women themselves might be physically abusive or
that indirect aggression occurred at all became irrelevant. What was
also lost was the idea that women in abusive relationships did not necessarily want the legal reaction mainstream feminists had tailored for
them, nor did they believe that they were blameless.

Given the overwhelming evidence of women's emotional and physical abuse toward others, how have mainstream feminists maintained
their conviction that these powerful findings should be ignored? How
have they developed, so vehemently, the view that domestic violence
is one-sided and male, and not part of a dynamic between two people?

To answer, I will offer a brief history of the deliberate effort by the
battered women's movement to separate severe physical male-oriented
violence that could or did result in injury from insignificant female
physical or emotional abuse for the ultimate goal of criminalizing domestic abuse. This move, as I will describe it, contributed a great deal
to the view that what mattered was the concrete manifestation of abuse
in the form of injury. Since men were much more likely to injure
women,[44] and hence come within the criminal law's judgmental gaze,
women's expressions of abuse, both physical and emotional, could be
both minimized and ignored.

This minimization was consistent with gender stereotypes (a holdover from the 1950s) that asserted the view that women were both
physically weak and emotionally subservient to men and were there-

fore incapable of emotional, let alone physical, harm. Any aggression by women—physical or emotional—was insignificant compared with men's violence. Moreover, women's physical violence was only one of two things: if it was severe, it was defensive; if it was not severe, it was not to be taken seriously. Physical abuse by women was often seen by men as less serious, and perhaps more like a joke or, at most, an emotional outburst. For example, Goodyear-Smith and Laidlaw found that men were reluctant to characterize slaps, hits, and punches from women as "assaultive."[45] They also found that of the 144 men who reported being the subject of violent acts by female partners, only 14 of those considered the women's acts as assaultive or "deliberately intended to harm."[46] Because these attitudes held by men about women's aggression resonated with what the culture still largely believed, people held on to these gendered assumptions and embraced the feminist stand on domestic violence, which asserted men's exclusive role in committing it.

THE SEPARATION OF EMOTIONAL AND PHYSICAL ABUSE

Despite strong cultural tenets that deny the importance of women's aggression, both physical and emotional, there is now little doubt that the wounds, physical *or* emotional, caused by abuse by an intimate partner can be deep and long-lasting. Indeed, some scholars have suggested that emotional abuse can have a more enduring effect on the psyche than physical abuse.[47] We also know that emotional abuse can cause people to become physically violent;[48] physical abuse can create an environment fraught with emotional upheaval.[49] Studies of reformed batterers suggest that although many men can stop physically abusing their partners, they are often unable to control their emotionally abusive tendencies.[50] Studies of women's aggression suggest that emotional abuse is one of women's most powerful weapons.[51] If emotional abuse is such an integral part of physical violence, and even an independent threat, then why has it been completely ignored by the law?

Elizabeth Schneider, a law professor, documents the history of feminist lawmaking in the area of domestic violence and offers an explanation for why emotional abuse was never incorporated into legal reform efforts. She finds that although there was some desire by mainstream feminists to include emotional abuse in domestic violence doctrine, feminist advocates ultimately capitulated to the path of reform that was most likely to guarantee success. Emotional abuse was too broad and unwieldy for the law. By focusing on physical violence, feminists found there was real promise for achieving the legal reform they desired. Because physical violence was already a common element of existing criminal law, there was less involved in extending its reach to the intimate sphere. Emotional abuse, on the other hand, posed particular difficulty because it was not easily defined or quantified. Schneider explains that feminist activists of the 1960s strategically uncoupled physical from emotional abuse to protect judges and the larger society from "the pain involved in acknowledging that issues of power and control are troublingly characteristic of all intimate relationships."[52]

The social construction of domestic violence, as we might think of it, was in part a reaction to the desperation women in abusive relationships and advocates felt historically as they faced the criminal justice system's indifference to their suffering. This was an urgent time. Women were being beaten by their male partners, and professionals, such as police officers and prosecutors, were completely indifferent, even hostile, to women's cries for help. To get the nation's attention, feminists had to be loud, unwavering, and wholly righteous. In an attempt to get the attention women needed to address the injuries inflicted on them by their intimate partners, feminist advocates defined such acts by their severity, by the injuries they produced, and by the men who caused these harms. Domestic violence involved violent men—batterers—and the women they injured. Whatever women did in response, physical or emotional, was irrelevant. The strategy worked. Emotional abuse, indeed, all women's aggression, was deliberately disentangled from physical abuse to achieve the instrumental purpose of legal reform.

One obvious by-product of characterizing intimate abuse as more "physical" than "emotional" is that policy makers, judges, and other professionals came to see intimate violence as exclusively male. Emotional abuse, and the physical aggression committed by women that was taken less seriously, was delegitimized. Women's most powerful contributions to the potentially abusive intimate dynamic were minimized. To further legitimize the physical/emotional, harmful/harmless, and male/female divides, scholars began to research the physical, injurious, and male manifestations of violence.

By particularizing domestic abuse as distinctly "physical," "harmful," and "male," for the purpose of obtaining legal recognition, mainstream feminists could ignore the reciprocity that so often accompanies intimate abuse. This created four distinct problems. First, rather than seeing domestic violence as a series of interactions or a dynamic that might or might not include injury and might or might not warrant the state's scrutiny and intervention, the problem was constructed as a crime between a person who causes injury and a person who falls prey to it. Second, by erasing emotional abuse from intimate abuse, women could neither legitimately complain about men's psychological violence nor take responsibility for their own emotionally aggressive impulses or reactions. Third, and correlatively, by constructing the problem of domestic violence as exclusively physical, and caused by patriarchy, men were prohibited from developing a language to talk about their own experiences of emotional or physical abuse by their female partners. Finally, by ignoring the possibility that women inflict harm, lesbian violence was rendered all but invisible.[53] Uncoupling physical and emotional abuse, harmful from harmless, and male from female, while elevating one over the other, meant that women were essentially removed from the violent dynamic and men were held entirely accountable for it.

I believe that the focus on men's physical violence that mainstream feminists advocated, for the benefit of the judiciary and society, may actually have been a form of countertransference called projection—an unconscious effort by mainstream feminists to distance themselves from the abuse they could not face in their own lives and from their own abusive tendencies. This picks up the themes from the last chapter, where I described how the countertransference reactions of mainstream femi-

nists contributed to their narrow formulation of women in abusive relationships as helpless and traumatized. There I described how mainstream feminists neglected to reflect on the rage and shame generated in
them when listening to the violent experiences women shared with
them. Here I want to argue that mainstream feminists projected onto
men their own repressed aggression while exculpating women.

PROJECTION AS JUDGMENT

The psychoanalytic term "projection" can help us gain insight into
how unconscious narratives of our own experiences of violence affect
how we judge other people who are experiencing intimate abuse. Projection occurs when someone refuses to acknowledge in himself or herself qualities, feelings, and wishes and instead locates, or "projects,"
these rejected feelings onto the other—a person or thing. This denial
explains how it is that some people see in others what they cannot see
in themselves and how failing to have insight into oneself contributes
to the refusal to listen that is so endemic in mandated interventions.[54]

Whether conscious or not, our personal experiences with intimate
abuse inform how we think about and judge other people's experiences
of the same problem. These ways of thinking, or narratives, evolve from
our own (conscious or unconscious) experiences and our reflections on
those experiences. If we are scholars in the field of intimate violence,
our narratives may be further informed by the theory and research in the
field, although it is likely still that we cling to explanations that resonate with our own experiences and the explanations we have developed to accompany those experiences. We do this because we fear that
if we look too closely at the experience, the event might occur again.
We fear that if we look too closely, we will realize that the event happened to us. We might also be afraid that talking about it will make the
memories worse. Currently, when feminists or professionals are faced
with someone who seeks their help and who needs to discuss the abuse
or aggression, they deny women these opportunities because, as projection teaches us, those conversations remind mainstream feminists or
helping professionals of the abuse they themselves have not addressed.

Two instances of how projection operates in light of our own experiences of abuse are worth illuminating. The first involves an empirical study of child welfare workers that I conducted with a colleague. In 1996, I received a grant from the U.S. Department of Health and Human Services to train child welfare workers in a method of intervention and assessment in domestic violence cases. Early on in the training it became apparent that the personal abuse histories of the trainees were influencing their professional judgments through projection. We found that the degree to which child welfare workers identified with their abuse histories affected their capacity to make decisions about the abuse cases they handled. In other words, workers tended to project their feelings about their own experiences of violence onto the families with whom they were working. Hence, those female child welfare workers who had histories of intimate partner violence and felt, in one way or another, that they identified with a battered woman's plight were most likely to understand how mothers in abusive relationships managed their complex situations. These workers were least likely to separate battered mother and child because they themselves identified with these women. Female child welfare workers who had a history of child abuse, on the other hand, and who therefore identified with the child's experience, were least likely (when compared with female child welfare workers without such a history) to understand the battered mother's situation. These workers projected their sympathy for the child in such a family; they cared more about the children because, I presume, as children themselves, they had wanted such protection. Workers with childhood histories of violence were most likely to be judgmental of the battered mother's decisions and most likely to remove the battered mother's children, placing them in foster care. Male child welfare workers who had been sexually abused as children were less likely to view removing the child as effective when compared with male child welfare workers who did not report a history of sexual abuse.[55] This gendered result, in which female workers with a history of childhood abuse believed that children needed to be removed from violent families and male workers who had histories of sexual abuse were less inclined to remove children from battered mothers, is highly significant. It is in large part due to the degree to which women view themselves as victims, an identity most men resist. The female workers therefore may have projected onto the children their desire for protection, and the male workers projected onto the children their belief that they should grin and bear it. What is key is not necessarily what the workers with abuse histories would do as a result of projection but, rather, that we take steps to make these histories conscious so that professionals can be aware of why they make the decisions they do. Perhaps, most important, we need to teach workers to recognize how their own experiences with violence color their perceptions of others' needs.

Another example of projection involves an experience I had in 2001 when performing a typical academic function—delivering a paper. I was presenting my analysis of the Brenda Aris case, described earlier, to an audience of students and faculty at a prominent law school. The premise of my talk, which is relevant to my discussion here of projection, was that one of the jurors in the Aris trial was so deeply influenced by her own history of childhood abuse that it affected her judgment in the case. I argued that her own history of abuse affected her judgment so significantly that she could not see Brenda Aris's life-threatening, ongoing experience of abuse. Her role in influencing the other jurors was so great that they convicted Brenda of second-degree murder.

Some members of the academic audience reacted strongly to my suggestion that the juror may have projected her own narrative of violence onto Brenda Aris. They believed, some of them vehemently, that decision makers could "contain" their histories of abuse, even obliterate them from their professional judgments. Interestingly, each of the three professors who reacted most strongly to my argument that projection explained the juror's attitudes toward Brenda Aris later revealed to me that they had been exposed to intimate abuse during childhood. Each also denied that their histories affected their professional judgments. One prominent law professor argued that it would take ten to twenty years to work through a history of violence in therapy; he queried whether we could realistically mandate judges to undertake such self-reflection. He admitted he was not prepared to do this work on himself.

My goal here is not to argue for the importance of therapy per se, or even to mandate that judges reflect on their inner lives, although I have argued both these points before.[56] My goal is to illuminate how personal histories of intimate violence become part of each of us, without our awareness. One approach—like that of the prominent law professor—is to deny that these narratives exist or are relevant. My alternate approach is to encourage broad reflection on our personal experiences of violence, in all its emotional and physical forms, despite the discomfort or time it may take to do so, and to think more critically about how even what may feel like minor experiences of intimate abuse are very likely affecting our judgments of others.

As the next section starkly reveals, we have all experienced violence, and we have all inflicted it. Seeing intimate violence along the continuum from verbal to physical aggression, a continuum along which we all fall, clarifies just how pervasive violence is and why we all have such strong views about how to address it.

THE PERVASIVENES OF VIOLENCE AND AGGRESSION

Let us start by recognizing just how prevalent violence is in our lives. Recently, the horrors of September 11 etched themselves in everyone's autobiographies. Whether we viewed the passenger planes flying into the Twin Towers firsthand or on a television screen, this image shattered our core assumptions about what we could count on in terms of our security and safety. Our minds convinced us that if such terror could happen in New York City, Arlington, Virginia, and even rural Pennsylvania, then it could happen in Los Angeles, Miami, and Bloomington, Indiana.

Yet violence was everywhere before September 11, 2001. It came in forms we have angrily accepted: serial murders of young girls, rapes of Central Park joggers, violent acts against gays and lesbians, and liquor store holdups. Violence also came in forms we have reluctantly acknowledged: violence by and against wives, lovers, and children. There is also state violence: the death penalty, lodged mostly against men of color, or soldiers killing women and children under the guise of "getting the bad guys." Just as both men and women can be aggressive, men and women can also be victims of some kind of violence at some point.

Consider the statistics on childhood abuse as an example of just how pervasive the problem is. Seven to 10 percent of parents who reported no instances of marital violence frequently abused their children. Ninety-seven percent of three-year-olds, 49 percent of thirteen-year-olds, and 34 percent of fifteen- to seventeen-year-olds experience violence at the hands of their parents, with 7 percent of fifteen- to seventeen-year-olds experiencing severe violence.[57] "Pandemic" childhood victimization, as David Finkelhor and Jennifer Dziuba-Leatherman refer to it, is violence that occurs to a majority of children in the course of growing up. Sibling violence, like the parent-child abuse just described, ranges, depending on the study, from 530 to 800 incidents of assault per 1,000 children, and falls into this category.[58] Bullying and emotional abuse by peers are also very frequent. In a survey of 2,000 children aged ten to sixteen years, researchers found that three times as many respondents were concerned about the likelihood of being beaten up by peers as were concerned about being sexually abused.[59] Finkelhor and Dziuba-Leatherman's typology also accounts for a small number of children who have experienced "extraordinary victimizations," including homicide and nonfamily abduction (.03 and .06 per 1,000, respectively, depending on the study).[60]

My theory is that we have all developed our own narratives of intimate abuse that correspond to the numerous and varied victimizations we have experienced along a continuum of aggression. Thinking about violence broadly, its everyday occurrences, gives rise to our sympathies with those we perceive to be victimized and our villainization of victimizers. This is what we have learned from understanding projection and the effect of countertransference, described in chapter 3. To summarize, the genesis of our countertransference reactions toward people who have experienced violence is deeply informed by whether we have insight into our own experiences of abuse or, as so often happens, we project these experiences and judgments onto others.

Recognizing that being yelled at by your mother in a supermarket has an effect on you, or that your lover's publically expressed judgments about your weight register somewhere inside you, helps us become aware of the deep impact of all forms of aggression on our psyches. Seeing these instances as important, even when seemingly minor, helps us realize something crucial: whether or not we acknowledge what happened to us as violent incidents, we carry within ourselves unexplored judgments about aggression. These judgments form the basis of our narratives of intimate abuse and affect how we think about the violence that other people endure or inflict. They even affect our reaction to other forms of violence. For example, they inform our opinions of the invasion of Afghanistan for terrorist culpability in the September 11 attacks, or whether we should dismantle Iraq's unwieldy dictatorship.

The purpose of exposing the often unconscious influence of violence on our own psyches is not to pin the label of victim (or perpetrator) on people who may not see it that way. Rather, my purpose in exposing the myriad violent incidents in people's lives and the narratives—repressed or otherwise—that accompany them is to learn more about how we have come to understand intimate abuse, based on our own experiences, in what ways we project those experiences onto others, and how as a result of those experiences and that projection, so many people have come to embrace mandatory policies as a response to intimate abuse.

Many people challenge my assumption that recognizing the universality of violence helps us understand it better. Most people believe that the experiences of women in abusive relationships are so severe as to be placed outside the realm of ordinary violence. Paradoxically, it is only by recognizing how pervasive violence is and our own experiences of it, however minor, that we can stop judging women in abusive situations and instead listen to what they have to say about their participation in abuse, however small. This listening, without projecting, will keep women safe, as I have already suggested, whether they leave or stay in a relationship. Furthermore, this awareness of our projection enables us to see intimate abuse not as one-dimensional but as emotional and physical, male and female, parent and child. I call this fuller picture a dynamic of intimate abuse.

PART TWO

Fixing the Failures

FIVE

The Dynamic of Intimate Abuse

ACKNOWLEDGING THAT WOMEN CAN BE AGGRESSIVE, even violent, takes us closer to the overall goal of recognizing just how much violence we all contribute to and are exposed to. My hope is that by developing the capacity to see beyond the limitations of the narrow labels of man as aggressor and woman as victim, we can begin to recognize in ourselves the existence of both of these qualities in some form or another, and their contribution, however minor, to a dynamic of abuse evident in all intimate relationships. This self-reflection is necessary to understand intimate violence better and to develop more appropriate and effective responses to it. To start, we must understand how and why violence occurs.

THE ORIGINS OF VIOLENCE

Several theories explain why people become violent in their intimate relationships.[1] Some scholars believe that biology predetermines a person's propensity toward violence.[2] More specifically, a child's central nervous system enables him or her to learn from punishment. A child with a dull central nervous system, the argument goes, is less fearful of being violent because punishment is less effective than with children with sensitive nervous systems, who react when punished and are therefore capable of learning to inhibit their violent urges. Recent research builds on these findings to suggest that certain brain injuries can also cause people to become violent.[3]

Scholars who subscribe to environmental causes believe that violence is learned from the environment and culture. People who are exposed to violence are more likely to absorb pro-violent norms and values, which, in turn, makes them more violence prone.[4] It is important to acknowledge that no one cause explains the pervasiveness of violence we witness or experience; both biology and the environment create the conditions for violence. Because my interest is in intimate abuse—its transmission and dynamic nature—I want to elaborate on the environmental influences and explore in more detail the myriad ways the environment can contribute to the reproduction of violence.

There is now little doubt that violence experienced in childhood affects adult functioning. Finkelhor and Dziuba-Leatherman document numerous studies that confirm that childhood abuse victims are much more likely to become adult perpetrators of abuse or to engage in criminal activity.[5] In addition, the same researchers found that children who were sexually abused have a "fourfold increased lifetime risk for any psychiatric disorder and a threefold risk for substance abuse,"[6] which we know gives rise to the likelihood of additional victimization and aggression.

In the realm of intimate violence, a clear connection has been made between violence experienced in childhood and adult abuse. As noted earlier, Straus, Gelles, and Steinmetz found that men who had witnessed physical abuse in childhood were almost three times more likely to hit their wives than men who were not exposed to violence in childhood.[7] Similarly, they found that a teenager who was physically punished was four times more likely to be severely violent toward his wife than one who was not abused.[8] Ultimately, men who had both experienced and observed violence in their families of origin were five to nine times more likely to become violent against their wives.[9]

Sociologist Lonnie Athens believes that a father's behavior and other forms of modeling encourage violent conflict resolution in children and eventually adults.[10] Donald Dutton's finding that batterers' feelings of anger are highly correlated with feelings of humiliation[11] is consistent with psychiatrist James Gilligan's observations that shame figures prominently in the violence equation.[12] The fact that Dutton documented one source of the humiliation in batterers as verbal abuse by critical mothers suggests the importance of seeing emotional and physical abuse as part of a continuum and a dynamic of violence that flows *between* men and women.

In his influential book, *Violence*,[13] James Gilligan argues that violence derives from shame. Gilligan does not actually label shame as violence per se, but, as we learned earlier, violence comes in many forms and packages. I believe shame is a universally practiced form of emotional violence. If we think of the most violent criminals as responding to "shame," we can even begin to see violent criminals themselves as victims of violence. The obvious interplay between the two—victimhood and violence—begins to suggest a method for addressing all forms of violence. If we could stop the emotional abuse of shaming as part of the abusive dynamic, we might be able to prevent other forms of abuse that are expressed in reaction to these shaming practices. Shaming is a type of violence that gets expressed in the power differential I described in chapter 3, and its effects are felt by both parties in the abusive relationship.

Lonnie Athens, whose sociological research has some parallel themes to Gilligan's, studied extremely violent male criminals. His in-depth interviews with these criminals, mostly murderers, revealed that they clearly responded to a shaming experience with violence, albeit violence that was vastly disproportionate to the shame they had experienced. Athens, like Gilligan, does not necessarily identify such shame as abuse per se, although both Gilligan and Athens recognize the impact of shame on its violent-prone recipient. But Athens adds a crucial component to this analysis of violent causation that helps us conceptualize more accurately the origins of violence. Each of the violent men interviewed by Athens had been "coached" by a role model who taught him to react violently.[14] Athens believes that we are all often the victims of shame or ridicule, yet we do not always react in violent ways. Many of us ignore these insults and walk away; others back down after an initial confrontation. The group that acted violently did so because they had been taught to react in such ways.

Extending Athens's theory of coaching to the issue of the obvious differences between women's and men's violence helps illuminate how and why these differences get reproduced. If we see the entire violent dynamic—mothers coach girls and boys toward violence because of the physical and emotional abuse they experience at the hands of men and women; fathers coach boys and girls toward violence because of the physical and emotional abuse they experience at the hands of men and women; and men and women who abuse each other coach each other toward violence—we can start to develop a method for unraveling and addressing it.

Learning to be aggressive is nowhere more evident than in cases involving battered women who kill their abusive husbands. Battered women, in these instances, are both victim *and* perpetrator, both guilty *and* not. When I first started working with Brenda Aris, I was struck by the contradictions apparent in her story of abuse. She considered herself a murderer as well as a victim.

"It was just like how Lenore Walker described it," she said. "He would hit me and then come back crying and nice. I'd have to take him back." Brenda told me she had no choice: "I knew it was his life or mine." At the same time, she believed she deserved to serve time in prison. She felt guilty for killing the man she had been in love with, for depriving her children of their father, and for taking a human life.

Joyce Bubello, Brenda's defense attorney, believed that her client was not guilty. Unlike the previous battered women Joyce had represented, Brenda "could not give as much as she could get." Joyce believed that "Brenda was too pathetic to be guilty," and she was determined to prove it. She failed, however, and after a long and controversial trial, Brenda was convicted of second-degree murder.[15]

On the surface, Joyce was unsuccessful in her attempt to persuade the jury that Brenda acted in self-defense because the expert at her trial, Lenore Walker, was prevented from testifying that Brenda suffered from learned helplessness or battered woman syndrome.[16] This clearly hindered Joyce's representation and may have made it nearly impossible to win the case. This fact notwithstanding, my independent analysis of the trial revealed that the problem may have been more fundamental than whether learned helplessness explained why Brenda, with no previous history of violence, killed her sleeping husband. When I examined the dynamics of Brenda's trial, through transcripts and subsequent interviews, it was apparent that she was convicted of murder, at least in part, because Joyce had unwittingly embraced the mainstream feminist view that Brenda was a dependent and helpless victim.

Joyce Bubello did not directly address the conflict between Brenda's victimization (learned helplessness) and her aggression. Joyce's narrative of Brenda's innocence did not, like feminist narratives on intimate abuse, incorporate the complex realities of Brenda's life. She presented her client to the jury as simply a victim.

Since Joyce did not let the jury see Brenda as both victim and perpetrator, it could not reconcile Joyce's narrative with Brenda's aggression. This problem was made particularly acute by the one juror who had a reported history of abuse and who was convinced that Brenda was clearly a perpetrator. The juror's strong but mostly unspoken beliefs significantly dominated and overpowered the other jurors who were more sympathetic to Brenda. Had Brenda's victimization and violence been characterized in a more accurate and nuanced way—presenting Brenda as both victim and perpetrator—the jury would have been more likely to believe her lawyer's account of what happened. Instead, Brenda was convicted of second-degree murder and given a sentence of fifteen years to life in prison.

What can we learn from this case in terms of our effort to understand the dynamic of intimate abuse and its origins? According to Lenore Walker, extensive interviews with Brenda Aris revealed that she suffered from learned helplessness. After years of abuse, including about 150 incidents of sexual violence, Brenda exhibited such symptoms as persistent intrusions of abusive memories, a numbness to the violence, problems paying attention, and alterations to her defense system. My analysis revealed that Brenda Aris may have been suffering from learned helplessness and even post-traumatic stress disorder, which clearly, in part, affected her mental capacity on the day she killed her husband. Yet Walker failed to inquire about a host of other emotional states that can coexist in an abused woman's psyche. I also realized by listening to Brenda's narrative that she recognized that her violence on the night she killed Rick Aris reflected much more than her dependence or mental incapacity. It represented an act of recovery and resilience, even an act of learned aggression. Her statements to the police reflected this reality: "I saw the gun and said *that's the only way to get rid of him.* I leave him but he finds me." "If he's dead, at least he won't kill me. It was self-defense." "He beats me all the time. He beat me up tonight then passed out. *I just had enough of it.* Everyone here saw him beat me tonight."

Brenda Aris was caught in a dynamic of abuse in which she was coached toward violence by Rick Aris, in the ways sociologist Lonnie Athens has described. I learned that seven years before Brenda shot Rick, the couple had gone with friends to an empty lot to practice shooting guns. Brenda had never shot a gun before, and Rick took the time to explain how it worked. He explained how to release the gun's safety latch before shooting. When Brenda sat behind Rick and prepared to shoot him on the night she killed him, at first the gun did not respond. Then Brenda remembered Rick's shooting lesson and released the safety latch; this set off the round of bullets that killed him. Rick had clearly coached Brenda toward the violence she inflicted on him; indeed, he had shown her how to use the gun that killed him.

The idea that Brenda had been coached toward violence may explain its origins, but does not explain how or why the couple's dynamic over eleven years of marriage was so abusive. Over the past few years, several researchers have studied the idea that certain attachment styles, when combined in the form of a dynamic between two people, can give rise to violence. The Aris case illustrates this point.

Attachment is the process by which one "attaches" to another human being in an intimate relationship. Adult attachment styles are directly linked to the ways attachment was modeled in a person's family of origin. Bookwala describes these styles and draws on the work of Kim Bartholomew[17] as follows:

> There are four distinct types of adult attachment styles: "secure," "dismissing," "preoccupied" (also referred to as anxious-ambivalent), and fearful (also known as "avoidant"). Secure types, in general, have a positive view of themselves and others. Dismissing types have a positive

view of themselves and a more negative view of others. Preoccupied personality types have a negative view of themselves, in general, and a more positive view of others. Finally, fearful types have a negative view of both themselves and others. From this formulation, it becomes evident that certain types of attachment styles might clash in intimate relationships. For example, a secure type usually functions well in close, intimate relationships, whereas dismissing individuals feel that intimacy is not necessary or important. Preoccupied or anxious types tend to be very dependent in intimate relationships, and people who are fearful tend to be distrustful, even uncomfortable, in the face of intimacy.[18]

In a study from 2002, Bookwala found that individuals with certain types of attachment styles were predisposed toward aggression. Her study examined both expressed and received aggression—in other words, the attachment styles of both the identified aggressor in the relationship and the identified victim. Bookwala found that people who were more likely to perceive their partner as preoccupied with attachment reported that they expressed more aggression toward their partners. In addition, she found that when a preoccupied attachment type was paired with another preoccupied attachment type, the propensity for violence was increased.[19] This finding confirmed earlier evidence that preoccupied attachment styles (those who expressed anxiety regarding possible abandonment) were more likely to be associated with aggression.[20] Another volatile combination was that of a partner with a secure attachment style and a partner with a dismissive attachment style. Bookwala noted that although people who are "secure" are in general less aggressive, they may become inclined toward aggression when they feel prevented by a dismissive partner from achieving the closeness they desire.[21]

The strongest predictor of aggression in Bookwala's study, however, was the pairing of one partner of the fearful attachment type and the other of the preoccupied attachment type.[22] These findings were consistent with an earlier study by Roberts and Noller, who found that the combination of a person with a preoccupied personality (someone who tends to be dependent in intimate relationships) and a partner who was uncomfortable with intimacy (traits of a fearful personality style) increased levels of aggression in the relationship.[23] According to Bookwala: "The mismatch of strong needs for intimacy and anxiety over abandonment of the more preoccupied partner versus the persistent tendency to avoid intimacy and maintain emotional detachment of the fearful respondent may make such partnerships especially vulnerable to aggressive encounters."[24]

Brenda and Rick Aris clearly fit this pattern of attachment. Rick was severely abused as a child by a father who coached his son toward violence. Rick learned early on that attachment was not necessarily safe and probably developed a fear of it. Although many of Rick's friends described him as confident and outgoing, Brenda was aware that he was often confronted by his own self-hatred and also had a great deal of disdain for others. On numerous occasions, Brenda witnessed how Rick's father would denigrate Rick, especially in front of family and friends. In childhood, Rick's father would literally beat this message into him, causing Rick to become both afraid of intimacy and also ambivalent toward it.

Brenda, on the other hand, was an anxious dependent type who had a negative view of herself and a more positive view of others, Rick Aris included. She grew up in an alcoholic family where she could never fully trust that her parents would in any way be there for her, yet she yearned for their attention. Intimacy with a partner, especially a partner who was violent toward her, encouraged her to cling to him, even when he rejected her out of his own fear of intimacy. This only made Rick more ambivalent and angry toward her.

What becomes clear from the research is that the origins of violence in intimate relationships can emanate from numerous sources and that children and adults can learn to become violent. Now let us explore in more detail how a violent dynamic takes expression.

WHAT A VIOLENT DYNAMIC TYPICALLY LOOKS LIKE

We have now learned that victimization and violence can be inextricably linked through environmental influences that cross generations. The question remains, however, of how a typical dynamic of abuse gets acted out between two people, and why it is so difficult to grasp this reality. Relinquishing stereotypes about women as passive and weak is a critical step in recognizing more concretely how a dynamic of intimate abuse works. Women's violence is often minimized or dismissed as horseplay.[25] As we have seen, feminists themselves have often relied on these stereotypes to minimize the significance of female aggression. Mandatory arrest and prosecution policies reinforce these stereotypes by assuming that women are the weaker party and therefore need and warrant the state's protection.

The extent to which women are viewed as helpless and submissive is apparent in feminist research, which is the source of the mainstream feminist theories I have described. A central theme in mainstream feminist research is to minimize men's accounts of women's aggression. "Nagging," "going on and on," or "failing to 'shut up'" as described by violent men, is universally interpreted as an excuse for violence and always dismissed as irrelevant to the man's provocation.[26] Instead, mainstream feminists' views of women's aggression can be summarized in three simple principles: the man is in control; the man is in denial of this control; and the man is without insight into the violence he inflicts and feels entitled to express it. If only, these mainstream feminist researchers argue, the abuser could realize he is solely responsible for the violent dynamic, he could see and mend his evil ways.

Differences between men's and women's reports of the prevalence and frequency of violence and of their respective injuries only serve to reinforce the mainstream feminist assumption that the man is all-powerful in the relationship. Men consistently report that they inflict less violence and fewer injuries on their female partners than women report, even when women are interviewed about the same violent incidents.[27] The conclusion reached by mainstream feminist researchers is that men tend to minimize their violent actions, whereas women are assumed to have accurately portrayed the violence inflicted on them. But what if both narratives are accurate? What if men really do feel that women cause them to become violent because "women complain too much and nag and harass them for no good reason"?[28]

Researchers Eisikovits and Buchbinder[29] confirm that these feelings not only are present in the abusive relationship but also represent an important feature of the dynamic of initimate abuse.[30] Although, on the surface, the male partner appears in control, and the female partner appears under his control, the reality is much more complicated. His "attempts to control [her] may lead the woman either toward managing the violence or to taking on a violent identity."[31] Complaining, nagging, and harassing may be learned reactions to his control or a features of the woman's attachment style. They might also be the female partner's way of not being able to ask for what she wants from the relationship. This, in turn, can lead the male partner to experience what Donald Dutton calls abandonment anxiety.

From Dutton's research we learn that men who experienced abandonment, either because the women pulled away emotionally or could not move closer for one reason or another, often became aggressive against their female partners in reaction to their experiences of abandonment. According to Dutton, "For assaultive males, the psychological and behavioral result of the perceived loss of the female produces panic and hysterical aggression."[32] Taking these findings one step further, it becomes apparent that when a man experiences abandonment in the face of a woman's complaints and nagging, this may initiate his violence.

If men feel women cause them to become violent, we need to hear them out and evaluate whether their complaints may have some merit, without blaming women for men's abuse. Letting women take responsibility for whatever aggression they bring to the relationship can only serve to strengthen their position of insight, action, and power in the relationship overall. This power, as we learned earlier, can improve not only a woman's emotional well-being but also her physical safety. The Intimate Abuse Circles described in chapter 6 develop a process for discussing these dynamics between partners.

I must emphasize that I am not arguing that women in abusive relationships are responsible for the beatings they receive, that they are to blame for the violence inflicted on them, or even that mainstream feminism has consciously projected its aggression onto the men and women who fall prey to the criminal justice system's mandated policy. I am not retreating from the feminist position that men should be held accountable for their abusive behavior (a topic I address more fully in chapter 6). I am only suggesting that an accounting of the dynamic of abuse that includes how women and men participate in abusive relationships serves the multiple goals of helping each of us understand intimate violence, minimizing the effect of women's aggression on others, and helping individual women make more informed decisions about their intimate relationships.

As the studies reviewed here suggest, men's violence does not happen in a vacuum. Violence is a dynamic that includes more or less significant forms of emotional and physical abuse. Attempts to separate men's and women's aggression, even for the lofty feminist goal of protecting physically abused women, only serve to reinforce the violence rather than to address it. Because female aggression is part of a dynamic of intimate violence, it is time to take the very important step of examining that dynamic and the projection that may have caused the blindness in the first place. Mainstream feminists' one-sided characterization of men's violence—especially their move to separate physical from emotional abuse, men's from women's violence, mother's from son's aggression—may have been as much an emotional imperative (the need to locate their own abusive tendencies in others) as it was a legal and political one.

We can conceptualize violence in a new way, one that takes account of women's injuries and also the possibility, or even the likelihood, that women's behavior might be contributing to the violent dynamic. This would be a radical formulation of a feminist reading of intimate violence. It frees women to see themselves as much as agents as they are victims in the intimate sphere and opens up the possibility that women will reject traditional roles and experiment with new identities. If we see violence as a dynamic—both genders can be aggressors—we gain an opportunity to reconsider the violence in which we are all involved and rethink methods for addressing it.

WHERE DO WE GO FROM HERE?

Although mainstream feminist theory and research have consistently argued for the overriding importance of male dominance as an explanation of intimate abuse, a more complex picture emerges from a review of the studies on the origins and transmission of intimate violence. Violence can no longer be viewed as a one-sided trait of one gender or as divorced from the other myriad childhood experiences that influence people's overall functioning. Looking at the bonds forged between people that account for childhood histories of abuse and attachment styles helps us understand the dynamic nature of aggression. And women's role in this violent dynamic is integral and must be examined.

We should incorporate everyone, especially women, more fully into how we view intimate violence and force ourselves to take responsibility for our judgments of others. This will help reveal what aspects of our own histories we reject in ourselves and project onto others. One of the reasons a feminist interpretation of intimate abuse is so appealing is that we can avoid doing this work on ourselves and instead place our anger or repression about our victimization or our embarrassment about our own aggression on other people. Rather than viewing self-reflection and responsibility as self-blame, as mainstream feminism suggests, I believe that by taking stock of the fluid identities of victim and abuser, women can reassert their agency and overcome the subordination endemic to passivity and acceptance.

As a feminist, I want to underscore the importance of seeing violence as a dynamic and to suggest that reducing violence against women rests on our capacity as feminists to recast how we think about intimate abuse. I am unsatisfied by the mainstream feminist argument that women's violence is somehow excused because it is defensive. I am unsatisfied with the mainstream feminist effort to minimize women's violence by elevating men's violence. I am unsatisfied that violence against women is seen only as male exertions of power and control, and I am unsatisfied that women are viewed only as victims—that violence in intimate relationships by men and women has not yet been understood as inextricably intertwined. I am unsatisfied that this narrow-mindedness is advanced in the name of feminism and in the name of protecting women from men's violence. I am unsatisfied not only because I am concerned with the argument's paternalistic, judgmental, and even abusive tones but also because I do not think it serves the specific interests of survivors of intimate violence or the overall goal of reducing violence against women. Developing alternative approaches for the thousands of couples entering the criminal justice system, even for the most violent of them, that incorporate the notion that intimate violence is a dynamic is a topic I address directly in the next few chapters.

If we recognize that each aggressive or violent step can lead to a chain reaction of varying magnitude, depending on who it is inflicted upon, we can find opportunities for interrupting intimate abuse between partners and across generations. For example, we know that being a victim can lead to becoming aggressive. Whereas a "victim's" violence may be defensive, and therefore justified in the eyes of the law, its effect can be as threatening or dangerous as a "perpetrator's" offensive violence. Violence is violent irrespective of its cause or genesis. This dynamic between victim and aggressor is rendered painfully transparent when the recipient of the violence is a child who, in turn, acts violently in adult life toward his or her lover, or when a wife shoots a husband in response to his violence. With these realities in mind, it becomes clear that we need to do more than explain women's violence away as "defensive" or to make excuses for it. To view the problem more broadly, our goal should be to incorporate the individual biographies of women into the dynamic of intimate abuse.

To the extent that women in intimate relationships, through their emotional or physical aggression, are engaged in violent relationships that "kick off" a male partner's violence, we do women a disservice when we do not help them understand more fully what they may bring to the violent dynamic. Women already take responsibility for abusive relationships, usually in the form of self-blame.[33] We have a duty to help them develop broader and more nuanced insights into this dynamic and their participation in it, a detailed understanding that could help them move beyond labels and self-inflicted judgments.

Under current practice, rather than encouraging insight, we reinforce in women the perception of them as victims. In response to their self-blame, we tell them, "You did nothing wrong." Additionally, a woman's belief that her violence does not cause harm[34] may have the unintended effect of increasing violence against her.[35] Similarly, we tell men that they are abusers: "You are fully to blame." They have no place to understand their histories of childhood victimization and, in turn, their attachment styles, their experiences with mothers or fathers who may have been highly critical of them, or their reactions to the shaming or coaching practices to which they became accustomed. If we took the time to discover how women and men understand their own aggression in the context of their intimate relationships, we not only could help them gain insight into it but also might help them manage the violence, both physical and emotional, directed against them.

A one-dimensional analysis of patriarchy justifies criminal justice practices with limited value, such as mandatory arrest and prosecution, that do not systematically reduce violence against women. When we see the reciprocal and cyclical nature of intimate violence—the dynamic—we can recognize the painful parallels between women's experiences of men's violence and the experiences of boys who witness or experience violence in their families of origin. We already know that men's violence against women, in many cases, can be traced back to their childhoods. Paradoxically, when viewed from this broader perspective, it makes sense that at least one study has found that men's violence against women is an expression not of power but of men's own overwhelming sense of powerlessness.[36] As we have seen, women also experience power and powerlessness in the face of men's violence.

These findings—the powerlessness and aggression of both parties—provoke an observation. Although violence against women may be palpable and real now, and therefore warrant attention, it is no more important than a man's exposure to violence in childhood. Perhaps if a grown man's violence is an expression of the helplessness he felt in childhood, it is as defensive an expression of violence as women's defensive aggression toward men. If this is the case, the mainstream feminist argument that women's defensive violence should somehow be considered less important (if relevant at all) than the violence inflicted on women by men might also be applied to men who are reacting violently to their childhood experiences. This logic, taken to its extreme, would lead us to pretend that no violence matters because it is always defensive or a reaction. This would have devastating consequences. We need to find a way, as the next chapter suggests, to acknowledge—and ultimately reduce—all intimate violence.

SIX

Changing the System

GALLA HENDY MET HER BOYFRIEND (I WILL CALL HIM Bob) in 1996 while she was working a part-time job as a stripper.[1] Galla was the mother of three children and a home health care worker during the day. Bob was also a health care worker. Galla and Bob fell in love. They were both immigrants (she from Guyana, he from Jamaica), and they had a good relationship. In 1999, Galla gave birth to their little girl. Bob has been on disability. He has been diagnosed with sickle-cell anemia and had also had hip surgery, an operation that caused him to walk with a cane.

Bob was clearly frustrated that he was not working, and one day he took his frustrations out on Galla. She had left their one-year-old daughter alone with Galla's eleven-year-old son while she ran errands for their daughter's birthday. When Bob returned home and found their daughter alone with the boy, he became enraged. Galla was met at the door with Bob's anger: he blew up and hit Galla with his cane. Their relationship began to unravel after this landmark event.

The fights continued until Galla took their daughter and went to stay with a friend. When they returned, Bob was livid. Their argument turned on his belief that Galla was cheating on him. He hit her with his hand and later with boxing gloves, all the while screaming at her for cheating on him. Trying to get Galla to confess, Bob eventually choked her with a rope until she admitted what was not true. But the night's violence was not over. Bob found his gun and put it under his pillow, making sure Galla saw that he planned to sleep with it there. In the morning, he brought out champagne and later forced Galla to have anal sex.

Galla's son, aware that Bob and Galla were arguing, got involved. Bob threw the gun at the boy and told the boy to shoot him if he didn't like the fights the adults were having. Instead, the boy called the police on Galla's suggestion. When Galla saw Bob on the floor in handcuffs, she started to doubt whether calling the police was the right decision.

Under the current system, which in many, if not most, jurisdictions mandates arrest in domestic violence cases, little or no conversation is allowed between the intimate partners once the police are involved. Similarly, the police and prosecutors do not converse with either of the parties. Nowhere in the system is there any recognition that intimate abuse may be a dynamic, except perhaps when both parties are arrested. In the typical mandated arrest case, either the person identified as the victim goes along with the arrest and prosecution, or he or she does not. The defendant or perpetrator charged with the domestic violence crime consults with a lawyer or public defender in a system designed to fight for the least restrictive sentence.

Galla initially went along with the efforts of the prosecutor. She testified before the grand jury, although she found it humiliating to tell her story to so many strange faces. After Bob was indicted for assault, sodomy, and child endangerment, Galla went to visit him in jail. Like many women, Galla had strong feelings when she saw her partner in jail, and was especially upset when his illness flared up and he could not get the medical care he needed in jail. But unlike many women in the system, Galla found the prosecutors willing to listen to her. The Brooklyn district attorney's office helped Galla to fashion a solution that allowed her to continue seeing the man she loved. A plea bargain was arranged which included probation and batterer's treatment, and allowed Galla and Bob to live together again. When Bob was finally released, he blamed Galla for the six months he spent in jail and could not stop trying to get her to admit the whole episode was her fault. Although Bob reluctantly attended a batterer's treatment group, his rage continued.

Eventually, their relationship ended. What Galla and Bob needed, if they chose to continue to be together and share their parenting responsibilities, was a place to work through their devastating histories.

The Intimate Abuse Circle (IAC) process, introduced here and discussed more fully in the final two chapters, is designed to counteract the punishment-oriented trend that precludes dialogue between the parties. Instead, the IAC includes the couple's community—friends, family, and even children—in the healing process. Had such a process been available, Galla and Bob, and perhaps even Galla's son, could have had the opportunity to gain insight into the violence that occurred that night and could have worked through issues of anger, responsibility, and blame more productively. In addition, the IAC could have helped them address, very concretely, their related retribution and safety issues. Together this process would provide the seeds for the possibility of healing the violence. Intimate Abuse Circles provide a distinct alternative to the adversity and shame associated with the criminal justice system and should be viewed as a way of counteracting the current system's limitations.

Several activists have advocated against using restorative justice methods in domestic violence cases for many of the standard mainstream feminist reasons rehearsed earlier in this book. A restorative justice approach is viewed as either too dangerous or unwarranted given the criminal nature of family violence.[2] This reaction is predictable; it also contradicts evidence that these healing and restorative approaches may be an effective alternative.[3] My approach is drawn directly from these models, which, as we will see in chapter 8, can substantially improve the violent dynamic in a family, especially when the partners have chosen to stay together.

In this chapter I lay out some of the mechanics of the IAC process in an effort to develop an initial sketch of this alternative system. I end with an explanation of why the IAC would be particularly useful in a case like Galla and Bob's. Chapter 7 develops in more detail the underlying dynamic of the process—how all the parties would relate to each other during an IAC. Chapter 8 presents empirical support for this kind of reform. The description of the process presented here is only a sketch. The specific functioning of the system, including the precise legal ramifications of implementing the IAC process, still needs to be engineered.

The IAC process involves a two-step approach. First, an Intimate Abuse Assessment Team, made up of mental health professionals who are trained in listening techniques and assessment, is assigned to each case. The purpose of this team, at least in the short run, is to clarify the issues in this relationship and what steps should be taken to address the abuse. The overall goal of the Intimate Abuse Assessment Team is to assess the appropriateness of the IAC for these particular parties by evaluating whether both parties are participating voluntarily and whether there is any risk of lethality if the more abusive party is not incarcerated.

Second, an IAC is convened. It becomes a place where the parties, along with the Intimate Abuse Circle Team, made up of professionals and a community of friends and family, can participate in dialogue, taking responsibility for aggression and abuse, making plans for the future, and healing. It also provides a forum for identifying the larger and deeper dynamic issues that I have described.

ASSESSING CHOICE

The first role of the Intimate Abuse Assessment Team is to determine the wishes of the party who filed the initial complaint. All participation in the IAC is voluntary. Some people coming into the system would still prefer to pursue criminal action, because of the severity of the injury or the desire for state involvement, or even to seek revenge for their previous suffering. So long as the Intimate Abuse Assessment Team has conversed with the person filing the complaint and with his or her partner before the case goes forward and has described the strengths and weaknesses of the criminal process, the criminal justice option should still be provided, should the complaining party prefer it. The team will consider factors such as "ties to the community" in judging whether a criminal justice intervention would be effective, should that option be preferred. Therefore, the real purpose of the work of the Intimate Abuse Assessment Team meetings is to open up a dialogue about the abuse within the context of the relationship—to look at rather than away from the violence—and to fashion specific, individualized interventions that are most likely to result in a reduction of harm. For those people who feel finished with the relationship and ready to pursue criminal action, their choice to end the relationship should be respected. Respect is especially important to the people most directly involved in intimate abuse cases and should be preserved as a mode of relating to all parties involved.[4]

The team will view violence along a continuum of abuse and will identify the work each partner must do to diminish the aggression in the relationship. Thus, even the party that has done the greatest harm has a role in the healing process. Yet when the person who has been the most abusive requests an IAC and the recipient of that abuse prefers criminal justice action, the wishes of the latter party should be respected, assuming the Intimate Abuse Assessment Team thinks this decision is appropriate and likely to help the person exert a modicum of control over the violence. This is because the job of the assessment team is not merely to serve one or the other person's will but also to recognize the importance of safety. The Intimate Abuse Assessment Team can facilitate informed decision making by investigating both the potential for lethality, assuming incarceration is possible given the crime charged and evidence available, and the extent to which the injured party feels coerced to decide one way or another based on pressure from the more abusive partner. There should be a presumption in favor of allowing the complaining party to choose how to proceed, but it must be one that can be rebutted with evidence that there is more to this dynamic than the surface suggests.

Given that the IAC offers a chance that a couple may successfully reconcile, and this is something both parties genuinely desire, the Intimate Abuse Assessment Team should probably allow anyone to access it, even those couples that have not yet involved the police or otherwise had contact with the criminal justice system. It should be possible to allow complaining parties to opt into the IAC under most circumstances. Indeed, the purpose of the IAC is to encourage more parties to voluntarily get help even if they have not yet contacted law enforcement.

Although high levels of satisfaction with this model are expected, as discussed more fully in chapter 8, some degree of recidivism is all but guaranteed. This presents new problems. Should the assessment team permit people to try again if the circle process has failed for them in the past? If so, what should be done to address past failure? Perhaps the court could require all those people who have been charged with crimes and tried the IAC option to endure a minimum period of detainment after a second arrest before permitting an IAC to be put together again. This would depend in part on the effectiveness of incarceration on the specific perpetrator. If, on the other hand, a couple is allowed only one crack at the program, this could send the complaining party home with a degree of coercive power to back up new commitments, in much the same way that Ford and Regoli recognized when they found that women who *chose* to proceed with a criminal prosecution were most likely to experience increased safety.[5]

If a couple were to be allowed one shot at the IAC, should former parties be allowed to take part in the program with new partners? Allowing a violent party to avoid the criminal justice system only if that party's violence is directed at a new person seems to create not only perverse incentives but also an unsatisfactory method of escaping accountability. Alternately, the return of an injured party with a new violent partner might indicate a high degree of satisfaction with the program and a need for that person to address, in a constructive way, whatever conscious or unconscious behavior might be reproduced over and over again in his or her intimate relationships. Although choice remains a key driving force in the IAC process, the Intimate Abuse Assessment Team should provide constructive oversight to achieve the overall objective of reducing violence.

ASSESSING LETHALITY

The second responsibility of the Intimate Abuse Assessment Team is to determine whether the violence is lethal and/or escalating. This assessment, done in conjunction with input from all the parties, will also be factored into the decision about pursuing criminal justice responses. The team, however, will be aware that the hundreds of thousands of domestic violence cases pursued each year in the criminal justice system do not all eventually end in death. As discussed in chapter 4, intimate homicides are relatively rare. In 2001, a total of 1,034 women in the United States were killed by their male partners, and 295 men were killed by their female partners.[6] There is additional information that is relevant to assessing lethality. In a 2001 report to the National Institute of Justice, Dugan, Nagin, and Rosenfeld found that a criminal justice response can actually increase homicides in some groups. For example, a willingness to prosecute violations of protection orders has been associated with an increase in homicides of white married and black unmarried women. In addition, an increase in homicides of black women by their boyfriends has also been associated with legal advocacy.[7] Although some ethnic groups have reaped benefits from mandatory arrest policies, these results have been far from universal. The question is how to provide the best response to intimate abuse, one that is most likely to achieve the desired outcome of reducing violence between these intimates partners.

In some cases the task of assessing the seriousness of the homicide threat will be very difficult. Myriad typologies exist of men who abuse women,[8] as do objections to them.[9] Assessing a man's potential for lethality is not easy, especially when the stakes are so high. Although simple guiding criteria do exist,[10] the criminal justice system has not had past success at making this determination.[11] This underscores the overriding importance of the Intimate Abuse Assessment Team, which can review applications, apply typology research loosely given its uncertainty, and assess the likelihood of lethality.[12]

Take the most extreme example. The team will have to address cases of persistence life-threatening dynamics or the patriarchical terrorism Michael Johnson calls the most coercive violence. Common partner violence, according to Johnson, involves low-level violence, which includes the dynamic of abuse described earlier. Patriarchical terrorism involves life-threatening violence over which the victim has little or no apparent control.[13] The determination of whether a case involves common partner or life-threatening violence needs to be made on an individual basis. The IAC would be most effective in situations involving common partner violence. The team should more cautiously advise the use of an IAC in situations involving life-threatening violence because these abusers may need to be incarcerated to protect their partners and may not be helped by any amount of conversation or healing. James Gilligan's findings—that education can rehabilitate even the most hardened offenders—suggest that the IAC coupled with education might be an effective response, even to life-threatening violence.[14] John Braithwaite, in his description of restorative justice models from which IACs are in part drawn, suggests that it is optimal to combine restorative justice with punitive justice, especially when there is a chance that the restorative justice techniques will be unsuccessful.[15]

Almost all available research on men in abusive relationships has focused on one aspect of abuse that might be used to assess life-threatening violence: how the man behaves with regard to his partner. As we have learned, physical violence that causes injury can be a uniquely male exercise of power over a female partner.[16] In some instances, physical violence can be triggered by a loss of power and control, meaning that the person has lost the capacity to control his or her violence or to think about its consequences. Therefore, it is important to assess the use of power in the interaction between parties.[17]

Some feminist researchers have scoffed at the notion that men are out of control when committing violent acts, noting that responding violently in only one of many frustrating scenarios indicates something quite opposite to a lack of control, and that such an excuse blames the victim.[18] However, the control that violent men may perceive themselves as lacking may not be over their own behavior but over their partners. Since so much intimate abuse takes place when one person in the relationship attempts to leave his or her partner, it seems that the departure by one person is the most threatening outcome for people who tend toward intimate violence.[19] A person's sense that he or she is losing control over the partner may be affirmed by the other party's flight. This is the most dangerous time for the person who has left, since most intimate homicides occur during separation.[20] An expression of a lack of control and one partner's desire to create distance are factors that the Intimate Abuse Assessment Team should evaluate.

The Intimate Abuse Assessment Team should focus on two other aspects of the relationship, beyond the man's behavior toward the woman, when assessing lethality: the history of violence in the relationship and the personality traits of each member of the couple.

Among the telltale signs of elevated and more lethal violence are high degrees of belligerence and contempt between partners when speaking or listening to one another,[21] depression levels in the parties,[22] stress on the part of women in the relationship,[23] and increased domineering, controlling, and defensive behavior from the more physically abusive partner, coupled with high levels of tension, fear, and sadness from the one who fears that violence.[24] Additionally, as we saw in chapter 5, the attachment style whereby one party makes demands for intimacy and the other party withdraws has been shown to be uniquely predictive of the escalation of violence.[25]

Mason and Blankenship have found that longer relationships and those defined as more serious show higher rates of psychological and physical abuse than do relationships defined as casual.[26] As such, the Intimate Abuse Assessment Team should assess for the duration of the relationship and its intensity. Johnson, Lutz, and Websdale found that 72 percent of intimate abuse homicide cases occurred after an escalating history of violence, accompanied by some significant forms of victimization. Increasing entrapment of the women, often to the point where some felt unable to seek help outside the home for the abuse, was common in the cases he studied. Additionally, there was often a shift in the pattern of victimization, toward, for example, marital rape, often within a month prior to the murder.[27] As such, looking at the history of the relationship and the extent and/or escalating nature of the violence should tell the team a lot about how threatening it is.

Increased entrapment may indicate that the relationship has become irreconcilably violent; evidence of this situation may help the counselor to evaluate whether the more abused party who claims to want to participate in an IAC is making a personal choice or is under the influence of a partner who has threatened his or her life. The level of coercive control that one party seems to exercise over the other may range from very little to complete. At one end of this continuum one might find a couple that has had a violent disagreement in which the husband has made no real attempt to overcome his wife's will. Toward the other end of the continuum, as in the Galla Hendy case, one partner may have exhibited behaviors that attempt to overcome the partner's will, such as when Bob tried to choke Galla and then slept with a gun under his pillow. As was evident in this case, however, Galla's will was far from broken. The assessment team's job is to weigh and assess levels of coercive control and power, paying attention to shifting levels of control between the partners of the kind described by Foucault in chapter 3.

The Intimate Abuse Assessment Team should also try to determine the extent to which the woman has come under her partner's "control," which may indicate whether a longer period of separation is needed before she can speak freely about her options and evaluate whether an IAC is what she really wants. The team will also consider that in heterosexual relationships, women express fear about physical abuse.[28] As we learned earlier, this is different from men's reported feelings about women's violence.[29] These patterns may reflect gendered dynamics in which the man feels hampered because of patriarchal norms from expressing his feelings about his partner's aggression. Dynamics of control have also been detected in lesbian, gay, bisexual, and transgendered (LGBT) relationships.[30] How the partner achieves that control differs in the LGBT context, as does the effect of the violence on the injured party and whether helping professionals will respond appropriately to the abuse.[31] As such, the Intimate Abuse Assessment Team should be trained to understand the differences and similarities between heterosexual and LGBT couples.

In the end, the question is, how should the Intimate Abuse Assessment Team weigh the risks? Currently, arrest, and in many jurisdictions prosecution, is mandated, in part, to avoid risk. Theoretically, the state arrests and prosecutes all cases of domestic violence. In some jurisdictions, again in theory, medical professionals report cases of injury to the police if the victim explains that intimate abuse was the cause of those injuries. With this kind of universal response, the state escapes the difficult decisions about which cases would benefit most from a criminal justice response. In the past, several jurisdictions have been sued for failing to respond to a victim's cry for help.[32] Intimate Abuse Assessment Teams should be used to carefully cull all available information on the effectiveness of arrest and prosecution in each case and on the use of the IAC, including the likelihood that the people involved in this abusive relationship will stay together and therefore continue to put themselves at risk for reabuse, regardless of state intervention.

THE CIRCLE

Once a couple has petitioned for and secured access to the Intimate Abuse Circle program, the next step would be to identify and recruit participants for the circle. This is facilitated by the Intimate Abuse Circle Team. As in the Intimate Abuse Assessment Team, trained mental health professionals will oversee the circle. The Intimate Abuse Circle Team's first job is to draw the couple into a "care community." A care community can be made up of people who voluntarily participate in the circle for the purpose of fostering healing within the violent couple,[33] or subpoenas can be used to compel participation.[34] For example, subpoenas could be issued to bring parties in for a preliminary conference in which the importance of taking part in the IAC is discussed. Alternatively, only the most important participants, or only those who refuse to commit voluntarily, might be subpoenaed. Once potential participants hear what the IAC is about, they should feel free to decide whether they want to participate. Since most people are initially reluctant to "get involved," subpoenas can be used to engage them only at the preliminary stage, to encourage their participation. If, after learning about the IAC, they are still reluctant, they should not be forced to participate.

Ideally, both parties would agree upon IAC participants. In cases where they do not (for example, when one party wants to bring in someone who will only foster aggression through derogatory comments toward the partner),[35] veto power could be held by one or both parties or by the Intimate Abuse Circle Team. Another way of handling these conflicts might be to allow contested participants into the IAC on an experimental basis to determine their suitability for genuine participation in the process.

Constructing a care community depends on the needs and interests of the parties involved. For example, aboriginal people using these approaches have tended to rely on elders whom they believe have special spiritual gifts.[36] In John Braithwaite's experience with Eastern and Western restorative justice practices, community representatives, such as church leaders or respected family friends, with some training, can serve in this capacity.[37]

In addition to the care community supplied by the parties, the Intimate Abuse Circle Team will have to ensure the presence of appropriate outsiders. Experts will be needed to guard against "victim-blaming" and to help the participants understand the issues involved in the dynamics of abusive relationships, such as the role of alcohol or drug abuse in promoting, excusing, or medicating the violence.[38] These experts can help facilitate a full and unconstrained discussion of all relevant issues,[39] and they can help the participants gain the tools they need for insight and eventually for healing.

The Intimate Abuse Circle Team will also want to supply a trained facilitator for discussions between participants. Some injured parties (as well as other family members) may have trouble expressing themselves fully in front of partners who have not been tolerant of their views, and a facilitator can help alleviate the possibility of stifled conversation by guaranteeing each participant a minimum amount of uninterrupted talk time.

The number of people who participate in the IAC process from outside the care community should be limited to minimize cultural confusion and insensitivity, especially because cultural sensitivity is one of the circle's key benefits over the current criminal justice system. The outsiders must encourage the care community to set its own norms and create a space where parties of any ethnic, religious, or other group feel at home and satisfied with the justice they have received. In some cases, parties may find certain methods of communicating stifling and will want to use music or poetry to help explain their feelings. The team should be alert to the risk that a facilitator from outside the participants' identification group might interfere entirely with the sense that the parties are solving their own problems using their own specific modes of communication. This could lead to participants having less support for or satisfaction with the IAC.

Inside the IAC, both parties should be encouraged to take responsibility for their roles in the dynamic of intimate abuse. This mandate, which draws on the arguments already explicated here, takes into account the fact that we are all, to one degree or another, victims and abusers, and that the abusive, or more violent, party is likely to feel victimized in some way. One party who continues to see him- or herself as nothing more than a hapless victim, and who responds to the victimization only with anger, is not likely to attain the degree of empowerment required for functioning better or even for healing.[40] Exploring the abusive dynamic in the relationship is key toward working through and changing it.

At the same time, it is very important that the discussion of responsibility does not delve into victim-blaming. The purpose of the professionals in the IAC process is to help teach alternative methods of communication that encourage participants to take responsibility for their own contributions to the dynamic and to articulate the ways they have felt hurt or marginalized by the other person. Once inside the IAC, the facilitator should encourage frankness about past behaviors. In addition, both parties should be encouraged to consider very carefully, and to take responsibility for, their roles in the dynamic of intimate abuse.

The IAC can encourage candidness and honesty through a number of means, most commonly by offering some level of amnesty for admissions of crime.[41] Impending or possible criminal charges against one party can doom the IAC by making it difficult for the party accused of a crime to compose a personal narrative that acknowledges past wrongs. This is why the IAC will probably function best when it is offered after an arrest but as an alternative to prosecution. However, simply taking part in the IAC should not be enough to wipe the slate clean. As has already been suggested, there is some support for the idea that combining the IAC with the threat of criminal justice action (should the IAC fail) may be a more effective response for reducing subsequent incidents of violence.[42] Truth about past crimes, self-reflection, and, finally, human transformation should be the heart and soul of the IAC. The next chapter lays out the potential for such transformation.

One possible way to deal with acknowledging responsibility would be to allow different counts of a charge or different charges to be dropped, one at a time, over the course of the IAC meetings. A charge could be dropped on a certain date if the partner indicted with the crime offers full disclosure and admission of his or her role in the violence during that day's IAC meeting, particularly when this confession is accompanied by a change in behavior inside and outside the IAC. In this fashion, charges could be dropped or held in abeyance as they are owned up to and the party's behavioral change is documented. Ultimately, the IAC will succeed or fail based on the parties' commitment to change.

The ongoing threat of criminal charges is likely to create the most problems for those parties who hold the dimmest views of the criminal justice system as a method of dispensing justice. This is consistent with the finding that mandatory arrest can actually increase violence in some cases.[43] The threat effect of the criminal justice system is least likely to impact men who have few ties to the community. To counteract this effect and to encourage empowerment of both parties, each participant should have a say when negotiating the terms of all standard court remedies, including issues related to separation, divorce, or child custody. For example, each party should be encouraged to agree on the parameters of a restraining order for the duration of the IAC program, or on the time line and custody issues for a separation and reconciliation. Child and spousal support during a separation can be agreed upon based on the individualized needs of each party. If both parties cannot in the end agree on a final plan of action, family or criminal court could be used to develop a plan and/or to enforce it.

The unloading of hurt and anger and the acceptance of responsibility may lead to forgiveness on the part of one or both parties, which may alleviate the desire for a punitive response toward the other party.[44] According to Kaminer et al.: "Forgiveness is a process of integrating both the good and the bad aspects . . . of the offender. This entails a process whereby anger and aggression toward the offender are eventually tempered with an appreciation of the offender's good qualities, or at least empathy for his or her flaws."[45] The parties complete the IAC with a commitment to working on taming their anger, inside and/or outside the relationship. Intimate Abuse Circles may offer a unique opportunity to regain in the intimate relationship what the violence has so deeply marred. If a person is frank about the damage he or she did and takes responsibility for it, both partners can begin the process of forgiving and healing. In addition, the participants' examination of their behavior and the dynamics between them can increase communication and supply them with tools to ward off future violence. As part of the process, the parties will be taught methods for recognizing triggers for violence and more peaceful responses to them.

THE INTIMATE ABUSE CIRCLE
PROCESS IN ACTION

The Galla Hendy case depicted earlier in this chapter provides a perfect example of the kind of violence the IAC could address. Galla started to have doubts about whether a criminal justice response made sense as soon as she saw her partner taken away by the police. She started visiting Bob in jail soon after he was arrested. Her regrets grew as she became involved with the criminal justice system, and they seemed to solidify after she testified before the grand jury.

The Brooklyn district attorney's office worked with Galla to alleviate these hesitancies and allow her to have continued contact with Bob. After Bob spent six months in jail, the district attorney's office arranged a plea bargain with probation, which allowed Galla to live with Bob. If Bob abused her, Galla could call the police, and he would be sent back to jail. He was also ordered to take part in batterer's treatment.

As mentioned earlier, Bob resented the jail term and the treatment, which he felt was imposed on him. If the IAC process had been available to Galla and Bob, they could have chosen to pursue this path instead of going to the grand jury. Galla would have met with the Intimate Abuse Assessment Team, which would have determined whether the circle process interested her. In this case it is likely that Galla would have preferred an alternative to prosecution and incarceration. Of course, Bob also would have been involved in this decision. It is likely that he would have chosen the IAC process to avoid prosecution.

As for assessing lethality, there is no question that Bob had been reckless and extremely violent on the night in question. The fact that Bob had a gun and placed it in the hands of Galla's young son is significant and should not be minimized. Either way, Bob returned to Galla, their daughter, and her son after his time in jail. Returning with the help of an IAC is much preferable to the current system, which offers nothing more than a short stint in jail, batterer's treatment, and probation.

Such tools as limited orders of protection that allow Galla to live with Bob, but also to initiate police action should she need to, would be available to people who participate in an IAC. Bob's decision to relinquish his gun to authorities and his desire and commitment to taking responsibility for his violence would be critical to the IAC process. Monitoring Bob's lethality risk throughout the IAC process would also be key and would be made infinitely more possible through this ongoing interaction with the system.

Galla's fear level would have to be assessed. Her decision to continue her relationship with Bob after the violent incident suggests that she was managing her fear, as so many women do; the Intimate Abuse Assessment Team would have to confirm this. It is important to mention here that many professionals, in assessing Galla and Bob's case, would assume either that Galla was coerced into returning to Bob through threats or that she was incapable of assessing the dangerousness of the situation. That is one view that leads mainstream feminists to advocate for a mandated response that takes the decision out of the hands of women like Galla Hendy. I hold that regardless of her reasons for returning to Bob, Galla was going to continue to see him—there was nothing the criminal justice system could do to change that, except for incarcerating Bob permanently for his crimes. Without Galla's testimony, it would be difficult to obtain such a conviction, and, as the district attorney's office seemed to conclude, pursuing this case would be at the expense of the prosecutor's relationship with Galla. The office seemed to recognize that Galla was in the best position to report future incidents of violence, and that maintaining a relationship with her could help prevent such incidents or otherwise encourage her to report them. Knowing there is power when decisions are placed in women's hands, the district attorney's office maintained its relationship with Galla, respected her decision-making process, and extended a lifeline to her. The Intimate Abuse Assessment Team would operate along these same lines.

Once the IAC process got under way, both Galla and Bob would select people in their care communities to participate with them. Choosing family members or close friends, including children who are mature enough to participate, should be the decision of the parties involved. The group selected should be willing to participate. Its job would be to witness the responsibility taken by each party and the movement toward change. This process might involve Galla's accepting responsibility for leaving their daughter alone with her eleven-year-old son. It might also involve taking responsibility for leaving their apartment with their daughter, for a few days, without contacting Bob. Bob would take responsibility for his violent reactions toward Galla and her son, including the incident with the cane, and for the numerous violent events and threats Bob committed on the night he was arrested. Perhaps the shared experience of taking responsibility would help Bob come to terms with his own guilt, which he undoubtedly feels in some way. Together Galla and Bob could begin to understand how to build a new and different life together with the children for whom they were responsible. As is illuminated in the next chapter, Galla and Bob could also begin to understand the deeper underpinnings of their violent dynamic, their biographical stories that led them to tolerate the violence in the first place. The way they met—Galla was a stripper at the time, and Bob was visiting the strip club—already involved aspects of power, control, and sex that could form daunting dynamics in a relationship, and this would benefit from exploration. Although Bob may have initially been attracted to Galla when she was a stripper, he may have later found her job threatening to his hopes for a monogamous relationship. Without assigning shame and blame, both Bob and Galla could take responsibility for their own behavior in an effort to understand how distrust may have developed over time and how violence may have been the result.

The process of taking responsibility and looking inward naturally gives rise to an openness to rethinking one's behavior. The abusive events can then be re-viewed from this position; triggers can be identified—"when you said this, that happened"; and, perhaps most important, the parties can locate these experiences in their childhoods, or wherever they are most likely to emanate from. This enables both parties to understand how they may have projected their negative relationships from the past onto their current partners. This process leads to more clarity about how childhood or other formative experiences and patterns may get repeated in intimate relationships and what steps should be taken to interrupt these patterns.[46]

Should violence erupt during the IAC process, it would occur under the view of professionals and the care community, both of which could help address it, either as part of the process of recovery or through the criminal justice system, depending on the severity of the event and the likelihood that a traditional criminal justice response would be effective in this case. The IAC offers ongoing monitoring that includes a whole new set of eyes—the care community—whose members are both much closer to the situation than the police and more invested in this couple.

If Galla chose to leave Bob during the IAC, this, too, could be managed through the process. Rather than being left on his own to deal with his anger about Galla's decision to leave, Bob would have the IAC—his care community—to help him work through his feelings of abandonment and to avoid violence. Under current criminal justice practice, the police would be notified that Galla had left Bob only after a violent incident occurred (assuming she called them, or someone else did). The IAC process allows for the possibility of preventing the violence and helping Bob to manage his anger in a therapeutic context.

To understand how communication and action would be facilitated during the IAC process, the next chapter outlines what therapeutic skills would be important for the professionals and care communities who choose to participate. As becomes evident in chapter 8, this healing approach holds much promise for reducing violence overall and also for reflecting on and rethinking how we as a society respond to all forms of abuse that touch our intimate lives.

SEVEN

Learning to Listen to Narratives

of Intimate Abuse

THE INTIMATE ABUSE CIRCLE PROCESS IS PREMISED ON two core assumptions: first, that the most successful path to healing from violence involves a relational cure, one that includes other people who help reaffirm the couple's faith and trust in the world; second, that the professionals and care communities who participate in that healing process do so with an awareness of how their own experiences of violence can cause countertransference and projection reactions, which, in turn, can interfere with people's efforts to heal from intimate violence. These two issues are key to the success of the IAC process and therefore are discussed in detail here.

THE RELATIONAL CURE

When one has experienced trauma and not addressed it, there lies an emptiness at that person's core, a loss of faith and trust in other people. We live in a culture that does not encourage people to seek help from others; once they do, people feel publicly exposed and embarrassed that they revealed so much of their intimate selves. Mainstream feminists, through mandated policies, have successfully exposed domestic violence to the world but have not made it any more emotionally safe or comfortable to reveal these intimate experiences. To do so is to expose oneself to public scrutiny by the criminal justice system. The purpose of the IAC is to allow people to explore these deeply personal issues in a supportive environment they essentially design. At the heart of the IAC process is the first core tenet of healing from abuse: a relational cure. Susan J. Brison, a philosopher who was raped in a village in France, describes the need to "remake oneself" after a trauma such as rape. As Brison observes, this remaking comes "by finding meaning in a life of caring for and being sustained by others."[1] Healing lies along the very path that brought the suffering. It is by way of others that the suffering comes, and it is with others that recovery occurs. Without connection, the healing cannot be complete.

This relational cure involves reengaging the person affected by trauma with others who can help guide him or her along a healing path. Trust, bonding, and mutual support, according to trauma experts, are necessary to heal and recover from trauma.[2] The IAC achieves these goals through the process of reconnecting the traumatized parties with their care communities and with professionals committed to working with them.

Boys and girls exposed to violence in their households should be invited to participate in such a healing process, as should adult men and women involved in abusive relationships.[3] This reinforces the overriding importance of providing men and women who were exposed to violence in childhood with the relational interventions they never received and desperately needed. This goal of developing relational approaches requires a method for encouraging the "trust, bonding, and mutual support" that trauma experts recommend. Narrative therapy embodies these principles.

NARRATIVE THERAPY

Narrative therapy,[4] grows out of postmodernism, a philosophy that rejects notions of "certainty," "truth," and the idea that we can ever really know anything objectively. Postmodernism recognizes that there is no "essence" or essential being. Language or speech, as it is interpreted by postmodernists, is not an expression of knowing beings but rather a reflection of the larger social, political, and cultural conditions in which it is created. Meaning, then, is both tentative and uncertain. Postmodernism is fundamentally political: it reveals the unspoken gendered, racial, or cultural dynamics that underpin interactions. Deconstruction is the method postmodernists use to unveil these subtexts.[5]

Narrative therapy, which grew out of an approach to mental health treatment that was centered in New Zealand and Australia, was designed by native people who were interested in developing a therapeutic practice that responded to their unique cultural experiences and to their marginalization and the threat posed to their people by colonization. Narrative therapy practice therefore allows the parties using it to think multidimensionally about a problem such as intimate abuse, and in ways that honor their gender, culture, race, religion, sexual orientation, and even individual views of emotional attachment. This is why narrative therapy lends itself so well to the IAC process I propose.

Narrative therapy, in the context of the IAC, would use several techniques to help the parties, the couple's care community, and the professionals to uncover the couple's stories and to author new ones. These techniques expose the underlying narratives or stories of women and men in violent relationships, while also offering methods for authoring new ones.

HOW NATE AND SANDRA WOULD USE NARRATIVE THERAPY

A woman and her partner share a certain language about their dynamic that positions them to relate to each other. The man (I will call him Nate Stanford) believes that he is "king of his castle." The woman, Sandra Stanford, capitulates to the "king of his castle" story and has essentially accepted what Nate expects of her. More recently, however, Sandra has changed her mind about the rules she feels Nate has imposed. She wants more out of her life. As the demands of children grow, and Sandra's desire to work outside the home develops, she is faced with the conflict between her own, now clearer, desires and Nate's position. Nate is confronted with Sandra's resistance to performing the duties to which he believes they agreed. Depending on their personality traits, including their attachment styles and each of their own histories and narratives of violence, along with other cultural, religious, class, and mental health identities, their reactions to these conflicts will vary, all of which contribute to the likelihood that violence will become a part of the dynamic between them.

The discourse that underlies their story probably takes various forms. Nate, for example, feels entitled to a hot meal for dinner because he brings in the family's income. Sandra may have previously unreflexively agreed and "bought into" this discourse. This disagreement positions Nate and Sandra in conflict—and quite possibly in danger. When Sandra fails to prepare dinner according to his specifications, Nate will find no excuse from her to be adequate to counteract his "I am king" discourse. A colicky three-month-old, the demands of a new job, or even a dying mother may make Nate feel more entitled and angry, rather than less. Sandra's pulling away makes Nate feel more and more powerless, and this powerlessness causes Nate to lash out more vehemently. The more Sandra diverges from their previously agreed upon story, for whatever reason, the more conflict develops. Nate has unconsciously agreed to the story of his reign, which takes precedence over all other stories; Sandra has to whatever degree diverged from it.

"Deconstruction" disassembles assumptions that underpin the relationship between the couple.[6] In the example, deconstruction exposes the "king" and "cook" identities they have previously agreed to and prepares Sandra and Nate for seeing the ways they have accepted or rejected these identities. In the context of the IAC, Sandra would be encouraged to think about the ways she only half bought into the "I am king" discourse from the beginning but nonetheless went along with it in the name of family harmony. The deconstruction process for Sandra uncovers what aspects of their relationship she does or does not agree to, what she is now willing to agree to, and how her own new narrative (as opposed to the couple narrative) converges or conflicts in light of what she now realizes. Marking the ways Sandra acts out those conflicts through aggression or other means (such as refusing to cook dinner to his specifications) is enlightening for her and involves Sandra taking responsibility for her actions. It is also an opportunity to reveal the control Sandra feels Nate has over her and her control over Nate, as well as what types and levels of control, if any, she feels comfortable living with or asserting. Also, this is the time that Sandra can explore other influences—cultural, racial, religious—that might be having an effect on how she views the relationship. This therapeutic work done in the context of the IAC and under the gaze of the care community prepares Sandra for consciously recognizing their dynamic of intimate abuse.

Similarly, Nate would have the opportunity in the context of the IAC to deconstruct the overriding significance of the "I am king" discourse for him and to question the biographical meaning of his aggressive reactions. What is so threatening about his wife doing other things and not tending exclusively to his demands? Can he live with those uncertainties or not? If his partner is no longer willing to buy into the "king" discourse completely, is the union a failure for him? Can their original agreement be revised? How can the care community help him to manage this uncertainty? Similarly, cultural, racial, religious, and biographical history would be explored to clarify how Nate finds himself reproducing forms of aggression that he experienced in his childhood. Nate's ability to acknowledge and take responsibility for his history and his violence is key to the success of the IAC process.

As is evident from the example, deconstruction provides an opportunity for the couple to see what they have agreed to or rejected and to reflect on their positions, their histories, and their respective power over each other within that discourse. The purpose of deconstruction is to pull the curtain away, to reveal the dynamics that lie behind what they thought they originally agreed to. "Deconstruction is a process in which discourses are exposed and people's positions within them are revealed."[7]

"Reconstruction" is the space of possibility, the opportunity revealed from the deconstructive process.[8] Reconstruction occurs in the IAC when Sandra and Nate have revealed the stories and their positions in relation to those stories, and are now ready (and able) to reconstruct them in ways they more consciously choose. Reconstruction allows Sandra and Nate to reject cultural and social scripts, if they so choose, including the "I am king" discourse. Reconstruction enables them to deliberately and consciously reposition themselves in ways that are constructive and fulfilling, for the purpose of disintegrating the hierarchy in their relationship. There is evidence to suggest that reconstruction should involve energizing the relationship with such principles as equality and respect, for the explicit purpose of reducing the violence between them.[9]

A full discussion of their respective roles should lead to increased empathy between the partners. They can work together to formulate a "reconstruction plan" for interrupting the aggression that has characterized their relationship, developing trigger words or phrases to remind themselves and/or one another (if they remain together) of their commitment to change. If couples are going to reunite as part of the IAC process, and we know that a number of them will, they are better off doing so when equipped with tools to make their relationship less violent overall. Even those couples who decide to separate can benefit, if they so choose, from a full discussion of their history or, if nothing else, the parameters of their future contact, especially if children are involved.

This new understanding and narrative would incorporate Sandra's desires and account for the fact that her sole or primary task may not be to cook Nate's meals at a set time. In exchange, Sandra would bring in some income from working so that they could order food in more often. Nate would need reassurance of Sandra's love for him if he were to feel comfortable giving Sandra the movement she desired. This is where the care community in the IAC can be very useful. Members can help reassure Nate and encourage Sandra to meet her own underlying needs. Support can be offered to both parties engaged in the process of change.

But what if Nate is unwilling to reposition himself in this way and Sandra is ready to embrace a new narrative that does not include cooking Nate dinner every night as she has in the past? What if the threats of violence by Nate get worse in the face of Sandra's now conscious decision to change, or what if Sandra gets more aggressive out of her own frustration with Nate's unwillingness to change? The IAC process is critical at this juncture. Sandra may decide to leave the abusive relationship, and the IAC can help monitor Nate's anger and/or threats. Planning with Sandra and even Nate and their care communities

about how to end the relationship in a nonviolent way is key to achieving the overall goals of healing and change. This is how the IAC
process can help prevent incidents of violence by being involved with
couples through all stages of the healing process. It can also help interrupt the transmission of violence across generations.

Another scenario may present a different set of problems. What if,
as most couples do, Sandra decides to stay in the relationship even
though Nate seems unwilling to change and her reactions to him may
be exacerbating the problem? Under current criminal justice approaches, if Nate gets reported, arrested, or prosecuted for his violence,
Sandra is likely to align with Nate to protect him from the punishment
of law, feeling to blame (whether legitimate or not) for placing him in
this position in the first place. This is one possible interpretation of
what happened in the Monique and Jim Brown case. As is so starkly
apparent in the Brown case, none of the couple's issues were resolved or
addressed. If, on the other hand, a couple is treated in a manner that
recognizes the importance of bringing their dynamic to light, there is
hope that all forms of violence between them can be recognized and
understood, even when they choose not to reconstruct their relationship. Although with the IAC process there will still be clashes, the potential for violence will be reduced because it is understood, engaged
with, and monitored rather than obscured, ignored, and filed away.

HOW DO PROFESSIONALS LEARN TO PRACTICE
NARRATIVE THERAPY IN THE IAC?

In order for helping professionals such as lawyers, social workers, child
welfare workers, and health care personnel to practice narrative therapy
techniques in a way that is most likely to achieve the desired goal—a
reduction of violence—they must recognize how their own experiences
with violent incidents will inevitably affect the IAC process through
countertransference and projection. Self-reflection is the only hope for
counteracting the negative effect of these influences. Until now, we
have not viewed this insight-oriented work as important to the overall

project of addressing violence. What was important to helping people in abusive relationships was a previous experience of violence, not reflection on it. The experience itself legitimized the mainstream feminist's and the helping professional's work with a woman in an abusive relationship. What we now know is that experience divorced from reflection can cause harm, as described earlier. Countertransference and projection can no longer be ignored. Due to these influences, mainstream feminism labels victims as helpless, dependent, and ill. It assumes that women should not stay in their abusive relationships and that when they do, they need to be persuaded otherwise. It projects aggression onto men exclusively, which, as we have seen, is probably not the whole picture.

We have discussed at some length the damage that can be done to women when professionals countertransfer or project their own experiences of violence onto them. It is useful to explore here what damage can be done when professionals countertransfer or project their views of batterers onto men who are involved with women in abusive relationships.

Most professionals working with women in abusive relationships are consciously or unconsciously judgmental of the men who abuse them. Most people unreflectively follow the standard response that encourages such men's arrest, prosecution, and incarceration.[10] Although in the abstract such attitudes have helped move many of us toward an intolerance for male-on-female violence, in the concrete they have undermined how we interact with women in abusive relationships and, as discussed earlier, undermined our ability to reduce violence. One precondition for a narrative therapy approach is to self-reflect on the judgments we carry about men who abuse women. This self-reflective work will free us to provide an IAC process that allows both parties to recognize and acknowledge their abuse and embrace change.

Although professionals often think of abusers as simple, violent creatures, we can recognize that the women involved with these men see them as complicated; they see them as needing treatment because they want the abuse to stop and the relationship or marriage to remain intact.[11] Along these lines, the IAC process must involve viewing the person accused of being abusive as in need of assistance, if nothing else to affirm the woman's view that he is more than just the sum of his abuse.

In 1997, Paternoster, Brame, Bachman, and Sherman reanalyzed data from the Milwaukee mandatory arrest study discussed at length in chapter 2. They found that when the person arrested for a domestic violence crime experienced "procedural justice," subsequent incidents of violence were reduced. In other words: "When police acted in a procedurally fair manner when arresting assault suspects, the rate of subsequent domestic violence was significantly lower than when they did not."[12] Arrested suspects who felt that they had been treated fairly had assault rates that were similar to those of suspects who were warned and released without an arrest. Interestingly, the reduction of violence did not depend on the personal characteristics of the suspects, but rather on how the suspects were treated. It is useful to stop and reflect more closely on how professionals react to men and, by implication, women and the effect of their reactions on the abusive relationship. Examples drawn from typical cases help illuminate how professionals react in practice.

(i) *The Lawyer.* Lauren Fisher is an assistant district attorney who prosecutes batterers in a large urban prosecutor's office. She works in a court dedicated to domestic violence crimes, handling both misdemeanor and felony domestic violence cases. Most cases are plea-bargained, and most batterers receive a suspended sentence and batterer's treatment. This is often frustrating to Lauren, who would like batterers to pay for their crimes.[13] Occasionally, Lauren takes a case to trial. She has become especially involved in cases where children are affected by family violence and takes a particular interest in the children's well-being.

Lauren grew up in a dysfunctional family. Her father would drink and sometimes get angry and throw things around. She often felt powerless during these episodes but feels she has put her history behind her. Occasionally she talks about it with people she thinks will understand. Lauren has never fully reflected on her childhood, nor does she have much interest in doing so. Lauren enjoys doing domestic violence work because she thinks she is making a difference. She feels that her father, who no longer drinks, used to victimize everyone in the family. At the time (the 1960s), there was nothing anyone could do about it. Lauren is pleased that kids can call 911 these days and get the police to intervene when the violence begins. She wishes somebody would have been there for her when she was young.

Lauren is still very angry about what happened to her as a child and sees her work as a lawyer as an opportunity to address the helplessness she felt in her childhood. Should a case involving a couple such as Sandra and Nate come to Lauren's attention—let us assume it is alleged that Nate threw several plates of food around the house when he came home from work and that Sandra, fearing that Nate was going to hit her called the police—she would pursue it to the full extent of the law. Lauren would ignore Sandra's pleas for leniency toward Nate and would assume that they were her learned helplessness talking. Behind Sandra's pleas, Lauren would assume, are Nate's threats. Sandra would be viewed as weak and under Nate's influence. Assuming Lauren was in a mandatory prosecution jurisdiction, she would not develop a relationship with Sandra unless she felt Sandra would cooperate in some way with the prosecution. The only time Lauren would spend with Sandra would be what was necessary to enhance the evidence in her case against Nate.

Mainstream feminists who support mandated prosecution would agree with Lauren's reaction to Sandra and Nate's situation—after all, it is important to remember what Nate did to Sandra. Nate's behavior and Sandra's perceived weakness are all Lauren needs to hold Nate accountable for his heinous crime. If children are involved, the decision would be simple: they should be removed from this family.

Another way to view professionals like Lauren is to consider that their anger clouds their capacity to work effectively with women like Sandra who want to salvage their damaged relationships. Lauren is so wrapped up in her own history—and her view of herself (and hence others) as victims—that she reproduces the helplessness that she experienced as a child by projecting it into Sandra. Rather than viewing women in abusive relationships as more than victims, she sees them as weak and in need of her protection.[14] Because no one taught Lauren how to assert her own needs and interests in the sphere of intimate violence, she is unable to transmit those more productive and empowering messages to others. This is how countertransference more generally, and projection in particular, affects the professional-client relationship.

(*ii*) *The Counselor.* Now let us consider a different kind of professional. Darlene Smith is a counselor at a treatment program for battered women and their children. From the beginning, Darlene recognized that many of the women and children she worked with at the shelter were ambivalent about their relationships, and that their ambivalence caused them to become confused about whether to return to their partners who they believed were abusing them. Many of the women wanted their lovers or husbands to get treatment so that they could return home and resume the good parts of their relationships. Once at the shelter, the women and their children often missed their partners and needed a place to reminisce about the positive aspects of their relationships. Ideally, these women wanted to have contact with their partners by phone while in the shelter and perhaps even to see them under supervised conditions.

Darlene has her own history of family violence. She had been married for eight years to Jim, who had often been physically violent toward her. She was angry for a long time, and in the end, Jim's violence simply proved too much for her. They have one child together whom Darlene cares for on her own.

Darlene has many residual feelings toward Jim. She really wanted the relationship to work. She also understands that she had to end it. She has worked hard in therapy and has come to understand her relationship with Jim and how it affects her work. Darlene, although still angry about the abuse, views herself as an agent of her own destiny. She believes women have to make their own decisions about the violence in their intimate lives and that doing so will give them clarity and strength to carry on as women and mothers. That strength, accompanied with insight, helped Darlene make appropriate decisions for herself and her daughter. Darlene is comfortable, assuming she can help create safe conditions, aiding women in working through their ambivalence toward their partners.

Let us consider Darlene's reaction to Sandra and Nate's situation. If Sandra had entered the shelter after Nate had thrown the plates, Darlene would have used techniques that mirrored the narrative therapy process described previously. She would have worked with Sandra to understand why she had not cooked dinners for Nate in the manner he was accustomed, and which seemed to precipitate Nate's anger. Darlene would have discussed with Sandra how her relationship with Nate had changed over time. She would have been comfortable listening to Sandra's descriptions of her positive feelings for Nate and to Sandra's assertion that she was still committed to her relationship with him. Darlene would have worked with Sandra to be sure her children were safe and would focus on helping the family unit to heal, assuming this was Sandra's desire. Darlene would help Nate get treatment and also arrange for some supervised contact between Sandra and Nate, again assuming Sandra and Nate desired this contact.

Mainstream feminists would criticize Darlene for taking this approach and view it as excusing Nate's behavior and blaming Sandra for his abuse. Mainstream feminists might even believe that Darlene's own history of intimate abuse inappropriately influences her capacity to counsel battered women. In other words, Darlene's tolerance for a battered mother's ambivalence toward intimate violence is not protective enough. I believe that women like Sandra return to partners like Nate in the hope they can repair the damaged relationship. Darlene's capacity to provide options for women like Sandra and a process by which Sandra and Nate can begin to address their violent dynamic under a professional's gaze gives couples the concrete skills and related support they need to learn new patterns of relating. If women are going back to their abusive relationships despite the services provided for them and the encouragement to leave, we need to develop methods that recognize this reality. The IAC process accomplishes this goal.

Self-examination is important well beyond the examples set forth by Lauren Fisher and Darlene Smith. Without self-examination, most professionals would claim unreflectively that they view victims as survivors and that they view empowering the woman in abusive relationships as key to their approach. What is common practice among mainstream feminists who work with women in abusive relationships is that they are tolerant and supportive of victims so long as they adhere to certain stereotypes—they are dependent on the professionals who are helping them, appropriately fearful of their abusive partners, and deferential to the professional's expertise. When the women demonstrate independence—the precise state they need to be in to recover from the trauma—either because they express an ambivalence toward their partners rather than outright disdain or because they choose not to support arrest or prosecution, the professional reverts to viewing these women as incapable of making difficult decisions and therefore in need of protection.

These observations suggest that professionals should address within themselves three key issues before they become involved in a healing process like the IAC. First, they must be aware of their own histories of abuse, however minor, and understand how they might develop countertransference reactions or project that history onto others. In the case of women professionals who have experienced abuse and not addressed it, these reactions may involve judging women currently in abusive relationships who tolerate abuse. It may also manifest in extreme or inappropriate judgments about a man's abusive behavior or fear, that is, an overreaction to individual cases of abuse. Second, professionals must become aware of how they may have been involved in a dynamic of abuse even though they may be denying this memory. Seeing violence as a dynamic is a necessary precondition for helping couples understand how violence unfolds. Third, they must see the ways they have both inflicted abuse in any form and tolerated it and must understand the genesis of their reactions. What made them react aggressively toward a partner? What made them tolerate abuse from a loved one? What makes them reproduce those dynamics in their work with women and men in abusive relationships? With insight into these three issues, as well as a commitment to seeing how their own views affect their perceptions of others, professionals would be prepared to become involved in the IAC process.

THE OVERALL IMPORTANCE
OF SELF-REFLECTION

Narrative therapy practice assumes that if professionals and even members of care communities are charged with hearing how the couple formulates its own stories, they must be familiar and comfortable with their own. In doing so, they can see how their own experiences inform how they judge others. This work also helps them to become conscious of their judgments when they are making them, and to regulate when and whether those judgments are appropriate to the couple's situation and not their own.

Professionals could do this self-reflection work as part of their training for the IAC, but how would we prepare members of the care community to undertake this work? For example, if Sandra's mother had ended an abusive relationship, it might be difficult for her to watch her daughter continue to be involved with Nate. Or Sandra's mother may have endured a violent relationship for years and has encouraged Sandra to stay with Nate, despite the abuse. Either way, Sandra's mother would have to understand how her own history gets in the way of hearing her daughter's story, from Sandra's point of view, and prevents Sandra from fashioning a new and different story—with or without Nate. The professionals engaged in the IAC process would develop trainings for members of the care communities that address the importance of self-reflection and a method for doing it. What is so radical about this approach is that we start to value self-reflection for laypeople as well as professionals and start to develop approaches to intimate abuse that reflect not our own limited views but rather the views of the people directly affected by it.

The IAC process can be successful only if there is a shift in the way we view couples experiencing abuse. That shift involves incorporating all the therapeutic insight we have gathered thus far. Most important, doing any healing work well requires reflection on the ways we judge the people with whom we are working. As emphasized in earlier chapters, violence presents the greatest challenges to professionals and laypeople because of the ways we have been taught to ignore abuse in our intimate lives and instead to embrace the monolithic and distorted views of mainstream feminists. Seeing how violence touches all our lives along a continuum that causes each of us, in one way or another, to carry unexamined assumptions about other people's violence is a beginning point for being able to see other people's violence and to help them fashion responses to it.

The healing I have described depends on two conditions: a system that responds in ways that care about people's intimate abuse, and professionals and care communities who are prepared, both personally and professionally, to undertake the work of self-reflection by attending to their own histories of abuse, no matter how seemingly insignificant or distant. We need to rethink our strategies in light of the important fact that people stay together even when their intimate relationships are violent. As mentioned in previous chapters, coming to terms with this reality is not as simple as it may seem. Projection and countertransference that remains at the unconscious level can cause us to judge other people negatively and to dismiss the ways our own behaviors mirror the violence in others that we are quick to judge. The goal is to understand how difficult this healing work is for everyone and to set our sights on doing it well. It is our only chance for interrupting the transmission of intimate abuse between genders and across generations.

A new feminist approach to intimate abuse would no longer delineate how women or men should think about violence. Instead, the IAC process and the corresponding narrative therapy approaches would help both men and women to understand the power dynamics of their relationships and take charge of the conversation to address them. If we make this subtle but important shift, both women and men could develop the tools necessary to make their own informed decisions about the choices they might otherwise make unconsciously. This process is only possible however, when it is linked with self-reflection. A therapeutic approach not only helps individuals and relationships heal but also provides the foundation for reconceptualizing justice.

EIGHT

A Better Way

IF WE ACCEPT THAT INTIMATE VIOLENCE CAN AFFECT everyone, we need a system in place that can begin a process of self-reflection and healing. Several systems similar to the Intimate Abuse Circle process have been developed in the recent past, approaches that aim to heal rather than punish. Perhaps the most famous of the examples is the Truth and Reconciliation Commission, created in 1995 to address apartheid-related crimes in South Africa. Archbishop Desmond Tutu, recipient of the Nobel Peace Prize, chaired the world's largest truth commission, which was founded on the principle that "reconciliation depends on forgiveness and that forgiveness can only take place if gross violations of human rights are fully disclosed."[1] The long-lasting healing value created by the stark honesty of the perpetrators of racial violence in South Africa has been repeated and articulated by many of the families of victims who suffered under the abuse of that brutal era.[2]

Restorative justice, the approach that underpins these healing-oriented systems, is grounded in spiritual traditions that believe in the potential of human beings to heal. These models offer more promise than the punitive criminal justice system, which concedes that punishment is the only hope. As John Braithwaite, the primary proponent of restorative justice approaches in the West describes it, many restorative justice tenets are as old as ancient Arab, Buddhist, Confucian, Greek,

Roman, and Taoist civilizations.[3] At the heart of restorative justice is the idea of restoring victims, offenders, and communities, a process that is realized through "those who have a 'stake in a particular offense.'"[4] Restoration occurs when the stakeholders or participants come together to resolve "the aftermath of the offense and its implications for the future."[5] What is to be restored is left to the participants to answer and depends on what matters to each party. In this way, restorative justice creates a tailored response to the harm.

Using the South African example, although some victims' families objected to the exchange of truth for amnesty, the vast majority of black South Africans supported the process.[6] They had their reasons. Rather than sending the perpetrators to jail, they could garner the wages of the perpetrators to support the victims' families. Other requests from the families of victims included honesty about what happened, an apology, or the mounting of a gravestone. The fact that the victim's families could dictate even an aspect of the outcome in an otherwise violent situation helped them feel at least partially restored.

Restorative justice practices put the conflict front and center to resolve the problem, rather than the person accused of the crime. This means that securing punishment is not the ultimate goal. We have already learned that punishment as an end in itself does not often respond to the people involved in abusive relationships, nor does it help people move from the anger that is both the cause and the effect of human violation. This does not mean, however, that the person accused of the crime is not required to tell the truth about what happened and to take responsibility for it. As noted in the last chapter, using narrative therapy techniques can help hold people accountable for their actions while also helping to restore self-control. This helps heal without judgment or shame.

Although such an approach to fighting intimate abuse may seem radical, it is in some senses a throwback to more cohesive and community-oriented times. John Braithwaite describes youth development circles, one of the primary models for the IAC, as being an artificial method of bringing together the community that has existed naturally throughout history.[7] Indeed, some of the most innovative methods of dealing with intimate abuse being developed in jurisdictions around the U.S. contain some acceptance of the need for a traditional support network to help the woman and man work through their violence.[8]

The idea of letting batterers go free is sure to elicit some of the standard objections faced by practitioners of therapeutic and restorative justice who work in family violence.[9] As we have learned, advocates have spent three decades trying to convince a sluggish criminal justice system that domestic violence is a crime and, in doing so, created an entrenched commitment to treating it as such. But there is no intrinsic need to treat wrongdoing with punishment. There is strong evidence to suggest that women in abusive relationships may in fact be empowered by therapeutic approaches. Indeed, women emerge as leaders in group conferences designed to address family violence. Pennell and Burford, in their study of family group conferencing, found that women banded together to cross family and professional lines and took a leadership role in discussing and seeking remedies for intimate abuse.[10] Encouraging women in these ways can only serve to strengthen them and, in turn, to heal the family unit. As Braithwaite points out, family members depend on one another, and society depends on families.[11]

Of course, a restorative justice approach may not be for everyone, and as such it should be an option but not a requirement. It works best when understood internally and at the level of the individual, that is, when the parties themselves desire restoration for their hurt. Just as we cannot prescribe how someone incorporates death—the ultimate loss—into their life, we cannot prescribe how someone will resolve violence in their lives.

As we have seen, intimate abuse is a deeply personal issue that calls for the people involved to make choices about how they want to address it—punishment or healing. Without understanding that we need responses that account for both options, we will continue to impose our own judgments about how violence should be addressed and never truly engage the people who need our insight and understanding.

I am aware that this healing work is accomplished only when it is done voluntarily and with everyone's eyes open.[12] That is why it is not for everyone and should not be imposed on those who reject it, at least early on. Although I admit that healing is my preferred response, I am not yet prepared to impose it on persons who believe that punishment will accomplish the justice they seek. I believe that, in time, the power of healing—and the examples the IACs are sure to engender—will persuade others of its value.

It is important to remember that restorative justice and a path toward healing are not necessarily easy. Some members of a couple will have a hard time listening to their partner's story. Many will not be able to forgive. The success of the healing process will depend on whether the parties feel they are listening voluntarily or whether they are forced. That is why the process by which the participant's stories are told is key, and why narrative therapy offers such promise. It is also important to realize that forgiveness is not a requirement of the restoration process. Although some people will seek and desire forgiveness, the restorative justice process itself has been shown to help victims feel better about what happened without forcing people to forgive.

WHY THE INTIMATE ABUSE CIRCLE?

As the studies so strongly suggest, the criminal justice system has not found a way to adequately address the problem of intimate abuse. Although in some cases mandated responses reduce intimate abuse, usually levels of violence are not improved and may even make matters worse.[13] Further, the current criminal justice system, even with all its mainstream feminist influences, has failed to integrate women's voices into its methods. In addition, it has focused on punishing the person identified as the abuser and neglected the very important goal of healing both people. Under current criminal justice practice, a woman must make her primary goal the arrest and incarceration of a partner with whom she may share her past, her home, her children, and her future. If she does not do this, she is denied support from the system (which may go on to prosecute and incarcerate her partner anyway).

The goal of reducing violence must override the current tendency toward blame and punishment. We must interrupt the dynamic and cycle of violence, wherever it occurs along the continuum of aggression and abuse. As we have seen, people of any gender, sexual orientation, or age contribute to that dynamic and cycle. Deliberately examining our respective roles with regard to violence—any violence—will be the only method that can accomplish the overall purpose of any intervention, namely, to reduce intimate abuse.

The IAC will accomplish each of these important goals. In keeping with principles of restorative justice, the IAC will be devoted to healing the parties if the parties choose to try to do so.[14] The IAC neither pathologizes a person's devotion to his or her partner nor jeopardizes his or her physical safety. Rather, it recognizes how devotion and safety can be linked and helps the couple or parties make better sense of both emotional and attachment issues, regardless of whether separation is the choice pursued.

Contemporary criminal justice approaches do try to address the mental health of parties to a domestic violence case, with therapy requirements for the victim or batterer programs for the abuser.[15] The single-minded focus on labeling who is who and on separating the parties may limit the system's effectiveness. Men of color, religious men, and lesbians[16] labeled as batterers might be unlikely to sustain treatment; perhaps these groups find the focus on patriarchy in batterer's intervention programs inappropriate and alienating.[17] Since so many people are likely to find themselves reconciling, how much healing is accomplished in treatment sessions where each party complains about the other to fellow "batterers" or "victims"? These situations, at best, teach the parties how to thrive alone but not together and, at worst, reinforce each person's commitments to his or her unexamined interpretation of the violence, exacerbating resentment toward one another. Although women are more likely to stay with their husbands if their husbands enter batterers' treatment programs,[18] it is important to understand that if abuse is learned, spending mandated hours in the company of people who are extremely abusive can have the effect of reinforcing rather than reducing the violence.[19] In addition, as we saw from the previous chapter, if the couple chooses to stay together, as so many do, they need tools to understand their dynamic and to address the violence as it erupts between them.

The care community also creates a just response to violence by offering services that the criminal justice system cannot. Honesty developed in the care community can have the effect of mending ties with family and community members who have been alienated by the violence between the couple. The family and community, in turn, can have a role to play in acknowledging the abuse, helping the parties take responsibility for it, and in monitoring and preventing the reemergence of violence, in all its emotional and physical forms, should it occur. For example, family members can agree to watch the couple's children during a separation or so that one partner can have the job that the other part-ner has kept her or him from having in the past. Financial help can be offered, either by a wealthier participant of the care community or by pooling small amounts of money from various members. Nearby partic-ipants can offer their homes as safe havens or simply as places for either spouse to seek refuge from familial tensions before they boil over.

In this way, the presence of the care community can help ensure far better long-term safety than the criminal justice system can provide. There is no hiding reality from family members, neighbors, or other people in the parties' inner circle, especially once they have taken part in the IAC. A passing cop may not understand the bruises on a wom-an's face, but the woman's mother and sister will be sure to know.

This more effective, informal system of monitoring the relationship may also conserve court personnel resources. One of the criminal jus-tice system's greatest challenges has been to monitor the thousands of domestic violence cases that have been sentenced to treatment, among other punishments. The need for better follow-up with convicted bat-terers has led to more comprehensive monitoring at greater expense with only marginal success, using funds that should be spent on strate-gies that are most likely to succeed in achieving the goal of reducing vi-olence.[20] Care communities can be deputized to help perform these monitoring functions with greater success.

Intimate Abuse Circles can also help conserve the state's fiscal re-sources. Under the Violence Against Women Act, $59 million was spent on "grants to encourage arrest" in 2001.[21] These funds were allo-cated to police agencies, prosecutors' offices, and mainstream feminist groups to develop programs that promote arresting and prosecuting do-mestic violence crimes. These funds could be better spent on programs designed to address and reduce violence rather than on encouraging policies that have questionable effectiveness. As researcher Lawrence Sherman recently observed: "Until you admit that mandatory arrest is a failure in our inner cities, you won't get anybody to spend a penny on looking for other alternatives."[22] There is another reason, however, to be concerned that the state is not spending its precious resources wisely.

In a study by Edward Gondolf, of the 59 percent of women who chose not to use any battered women's services after the arrest of their partners because they "had no need for them," 44 percent said the services were unnecessary because "they had support from friends, family or church members instead." Additionally, these women reported that they were very "unlikely to face more assault and tended to feel 'very safe.'"[23] This shows the strength and support that a community of care can offer to women who have experienced violence in their intimate relationships.[24] We need to take advantage of these important and inexpensive resources and develop them to address violence.

Although the IAC has not yet been tried in the form I have proposed here, there is evidence that restorative justice practices that draw on the same principles do in fact result in better outcomes and more satisfaction for all parties involved when compared with traditional criminal justice models.[25] For example, in 1998, Burford and Pennell studied family violence conferencing approaches, which bring family members together to discuss abuse, including sexual abuse, in an effort to promote long-term healing. Burford and Pennell found substantial reductions in thirty-one problem behaviors, ranging from alcohol abuse to domestic violence, as compared with families who did not attend family group conferences.[26] In addition, participants found the family violence conferences satisfying and helpful: "94 percent of family members were 'satisfied with the way it was run,' 92 percent felt they were 'able to say what was important,' and 92 percent 'agreed with the plan decided on.'"[27] The findings suggest that people who participate in restorative justice approaches to family violence situations are surprisingly satisfied with the results and infinitely more engaged than the current system allows for.[28]

In addition, restorative justice models have been shown to deter crime better than criminal justice practices based on deterrence theory,[29] to incapacitate crime better than criminal justice practices grounded in the theory of selective incapacitation,[30] and to rehabilitate crime better than criminal justice practices grounded in the welfare model.[31] Restorative justice practices are more cost-effective than criminal justice practices grounded in an economic analysis of crime.[32]

Fitting the restorative justice model to the problem of intimate abuse may not be without its problems. Since the IACs do not depend on locking the offender away, they may increase victim fears of revictimization.[33] However, it has been shown that in other models of restorative justice, decreased fears of revictimization are twice as common as increases.[34] Having professionals such as the Intimate Abuse Assessment Team and Intimate Abuse Circle Team can contribute to the sense of power of the more vulnerable member. These professionals can teach the more vulnerable partner and supportive family and friends techniques like safety planning and other methods of seizing control that can reduce their fears of revictimization. Simultaneously, these professionals can help monitor violent behavior that is exhibited in the IAC.

People may still object to what seems like light treatment of serious criminals. There is perhaps a natural tendency to subject those who commit violence to the violence of the criminal justice system. However, it is often beneficial to choose healing over punishment—assuming the parties feel comfortable doing so. As one commentator said of the South African Truth and Reconciliation Commission: "Forgiving the perpetrators is a move that is partly magnanimous and mostly pragmatic."[35] This is extremely apt in the context of intimate violence. Healing and forgiveness can have numerous ripple effects: on the woman's expressions of aggression, as they lessen through the process of self-discovery and forgiveness, and on the man's expressions of abuse, as they weaken through the process of self-discovery and forgiveness. Perhaps most important, both parties benefit as parents by recognizing and reducing violence for the children involved.

Some people worry that the shaming that can inevitably occur when a care community is gathered together can worsen rather than improve the stigmatization of the more abusive partner.[36] The IAC members, the Intimate Abuse Assessment Team, and the Intimate Abuse Circle Teams can head off shaming before it begins by employing techniques that encourage the more abusive partner to take responsibility for his or her actions from the outset through narrative therapy and other liberating methods. Inviting participants of the more abusive partner's choice into the IAC is another way to combat this concern, and to ensure that the long-term goal of healing the abuse is achieved, rather than the stereotyping and labeling that are so endemic to the current system, which can foster anger and abuse.[37]

As we have seen, the criminal justice system has a long history of tepid support for enforcement of laws against intimate abuse. Mainstream feminists have tried to correct these problems by mandating arrest and prosecution. Yet these attempts have failed, largely because intimate abuse is different from stranger violence and, hence, less conducive to punishment-oriented approaches. We are all better served if we capitalize on this reality rather than continuing to pretend it does not exist. The criminal justice system may have more success at combating intimate abuse if it works for, rather than against, the wishes of the parties.

FINAL REFLECTIONS

My effort to develop a new theory and practice springs from my hope that by recognizing mainstream feminism's power to define the politics of intimate abuse, we can think more critically about it. Mainstream feminism cannot continue to use law as if it is a neutral instrument or a panacea. Law wields power as a blunt instrument; as Foucault showed, power is constituted in relationships much more than it is imposed from above. Of all schools of thought, feminism should be attentive to the relationships of power that law frames and must be wary of its own contribution to that dynamic. At the very least, we need to recognize that authority, including the authority of feminism, comes with its own history. Authority is imbued with the dynamics of countertransference and projection, with the fears and desires of those who wield it in relation to those whom they wish to help or punish. When mainstream feminists refuse to listen to women in abusive relationships, or refuse to account for women's violence, or reject attempts to broaden the conversation and dismiss questions about how representative a voice mainstream feminism lawmaking expresses, it comes dangerously close to using law to reproduce the violence it seeks to ameliorate.[38]

I have argued that although the oppression of women remains significant, perhaps in certain corridors as significant as it was thirty years ago, our methods for counteracting it have evolved. We now have the theoretical tools to think more broadly, and with more nuance, about the oppression of women and men. Principally, we need to move beyond the modernist framework within which mainstream feminist politics developed. Feminism needs to be attentive to differences and flexible in its offerings and responses. In particular, that means moving away from the hegemonic or uniform belief that there is only one answer, truth, or law. As feminists we know better, and as women we deserve more.

By recognizing women's aggression, we can think differently about women's power and agency. Women need not see themselves solely as victims anymore. It is unrealistic to imagine that abuse and violence can be eradicated from intimate relationships, and it does not help to formulate policies as if violence and abuse could be made to disappear. To get real about intimate abuse and to develop ways of coping and responding to it means taking responsibility, among other things, for women's role in perpetuating violence, in violence coaching, and in relational dynamics that foster abuse.

Finally, I know that as mothers we need to learn how to think about our anger toward our children and about the conditions in our lives that contribute to that anger. We need to fight against those conditions rather than reacting with anger toward our children because of those conditions. Each of us is responsible for violence against women and for understanding it and working it through. Taking responsibility for that task, as I am suggesting, affirms women's power and authority over our own lives. Knowing where and when our own aggression or violence exhibits itself or kicks off another's is powerful because it gives us the option to change it. And there is much to change.

Many people see intimate abuse more broadly than mainstream feminism has allowed. These people, myself included, have begun to call for changes in how we think about it. The problem is no longer just about women, as I have shown, but about mothers, fathers, children, women and men—about all of us.

On each step of the journey I have questioned my position, turned it around, sought input from those who would talk to me. I have struggled to understand what my motivations are, to understand them historically and biographically, to be sure that my response to such policies as mandatory intervention is not just a reaction to the entrenchment I have felt so strongly from mainstream feminists. I have tried to do to myself what I have done in this book: questioned, reflected, argued, and rethought.

Occasionally I would wake up, usually from a bad dream, and ask: Don't we need the criminal justice system to respond regardless of women's wishes? Don't we need to get men like Jim Brown and Rick Aris put away in order to prevent terrible violence? Don't we need a big stick to use on the batterer? In the cold light of day, I realize that using one approach only—beating the batterer and ignoring the wishes of the intimate partner—is hardly the route to diminishing violence. I took strength from women of color and lesbian activists who shared my sense of the coercion of these policies. I was consistently comforted by research that supported my view of the problem and by people who felt brave enough to tell me I must keep going, because my work was urgently needed to counteract what had become a hegemonic force in domestic violence practice and policy making.

As people working in the field began to resonate with what I was saying and, in whispers, to tell me that they, too, were worried about the ways we judge women when they return to abusive relationships and the ways we judge the men they return to, I became clearer in my convictions. Their voices were accompanied by those practitioners I respect who were doing treatment with men using mainstream feminist approaches and feeling stifled by narrow definitions of patriarchy that failed to address the cultural, racial, gender and class dimensions of their clients' lives. And women in abusive relationships have taught me the importance of focusing more directly on their needs and the reasons they find traditional legal and social work responses so unhelpful.

Perhaps it is my own journey back from an abusive relationship, however, that has been most influential. Nearly twenty years ago, I was involved with an exciting and brilliant man who worked in violence prevention. The abuse in our relationship began three months after we became a couple and continued until I ended the relationship one and a half years later. The violence ranged from a sock on the arm, to a push across a room, to spitting at my face, to rape. When we broke up, he stalked me. I know he still asks people who have contact with me how and what I am doing. A few years ago, he followed me to a public event he thought I might attend. I still maintain an unlisted home telephone number.

Whenever I reflect on this experience, I ask myself, what if the neighbors had called the police? (I would never have called.) I would have been mortified and horrified. An arrest would have ruined his life, robbed him of his work, and destroyed his reputation. I would have sided with him and lied for him. Even now, with all that I have learned, I would choose to protect him. Most mainstream feminists would say that is patriarchy talking, and that I still have not realized my feminist consciousness.

I disagree. My ex-lover was a man whose childhood was marred by suffering. His mother contributed a great deal to his violent reactions toward me, and I was conscious of the connection between his neediness and his "lashing out." Although at the time I did not see it so clearly, I could tell that his power was linked to powerlessness, that his strength was bound to his weakness. I also knew that I was young, naive, and also suffering, and I used whatever emotional resources I could to hurt him. Eventually I left him for a relationship with one of his best friends.

But it was only as I started to write this book that I realized that I, too, was engaged in a dynamic of abuse. Although I cannot specifically identify the ways I set off his violence, with the distance of time, I do know that we fed on each other's insecurities and dependencies. I fostered his; he reinforced mine. Given his childhood experiences with abuse, his violent reaction to my reactions and outbursts were almost predictable. My leaving this man for one of his closest friends was the ultimate slap in the face. My budding relationship with his close friend was also the catalyst for his anger at me the night he raped me.

With little help (three therapists refused to see us together and admonished him to get help on his own) to address these core issues, there was no chance that we would stay together—nor would I have wanted to. I stopped loving him at some point, and we did not have children or a shared cultural identity to bind us together. I was not dependent on him financially.

Taking responsibility for what I brought to the dynamic was a source of strength for me, not further guilt. I do not feel responsible for his violence, nor do I feel guilty for setting it off. What is empowering about becoming conscious of what I brought to the relationship in terms of my own aggression or attachment style is having control over my own destiny and seizing it. Knowing what I am capable of, and how it can get expressed in intimate relationships, helps me to be more thoughtful about how I treat the people I love, my husband and son included.

It has taken me several years to reach these conclusions. The healing has occurred in stages. Only five years after I broke up with this man did I recall the rape. I had completely wiped it from my consciousness, while I recalled other parts of the relationship with clarity. I remember that while the hitting, pushing, and spitting were going on, no one really understood the violence, and only a few people were willing to talk about it. I remember feeling that when I found people who could talk about it, they seemed very angry, especially angry at him. I did not want to be angry because I thought that only made the cycle more vicious. Mostly I remember the way I felt about myself. I felt stupid; I blamed myself for not seeing it sooner or more clearly, for not knowing ahead of time that he would be violent. This I could not talk about. Everyone would say, "it isn't your fault, it's him." Ironically, this only made things worse. As in the story of Sara, who lives at Ground Zero, related in chapter 1, I found myself feeling more anxious as people tried to calm me down. My "victim" stance, "he did it all to me," only contributed to my bad feelings about myself. As painful as it is to say, I think I felt this for ten of the last twenty years. Not until I could see my own contribution to the abuse in the relationship and to assign responsibility for mine and his could I free myself of that history and create the possibility of not repeating it.

Looking through the narrow lens of victim did not help me to heal. It was almost as if my years of suffering as a victim helped me realize how incomplete the victim narrative was.

In 1995, I visited Frontera Prison, where I first met Brenda Aris. I remember asking the members of Incarcerated Women Against Abuse, most of whom were serving life sentences for having killed the men who abused them, whether any of them still loved the men they killed. When nearly every one said she did, I was faced with a dilemma: learn more about these men, or lose the chance to relate to the women with whom I shared a history.

I undertook that risky journey through various means. First I investigated mandatory arrest and prosecution policies. In the beginning, I challenged these policies simply on the grounds that they do not consult the women most affected by violence. Then, to my shock, I learned that these policies were mostly symbolic and often ineffective anyway.

Second, when Brenda was discharged from prison, I tried an experiment. Together with a colleague, David Lewis, I brought Brenda and two very violent men together to talk about intimate abuse on film. All the participants had struggled to understand their victimhood and abusiveness, and it was powerful to see them interact. At times the male narratives dominated the discourse. At other times Brenda and I stood as survivors and confronted the men's attempts to control. I found that by allowing such a conversation to occur, we could all gain insight into intimate abuse. This experiment—like the Intimate Abuse Circles proposed here—must be continued if we are to move toward understanding intimate violence, rather than just fighting against it.

I knew that bringing victims and perpetrators together to discuss intimate abuse was controversial. I just did not know how controversial it was. I presented the film at a prominent law school to an audience of 150 people. Brenda and all the other participants in the video attended and sat in the front of the theater for a panel discussion that was to follow the screening. About one-quarter of the way through the video, two law professors walked out. I was stunned. I later learned that each of the professors who walked out had been a prosecutor, and each of them was horrified that I could bring perpetrators to their school to discuss their violence. These lawyers could not face, understand, or learn from the violence; they could only reject it.

The evening was emotional for everyone. Brenda's "care community" attended the event, and her therapist, who had not viewed the film before, was quite dismayed that Brenda had participated in a group session that included perpetrators. Brenda was not intimidated. She told the crowd and her therapist that the process of making the film allowed her to work through some of her anger at Rick, to take responsibility for her own violence, and to move her own conversation about aggression forward. She was glad she had done it.

Like Brenda, I, too, was confronted with judgment. A colleague who viewed the film recognized, from the description I gave, the man who had abused me in the ways I mentioned. She felt compelled, she told me, to disclose to my ex-lover that the film described him in a way that included identifying qualities. She said she would avoid this action if I removed the segment that included his identifiers. Initially, I was shocked by her threat. Eventually, I came to understand that this woman's reaction reflected her sympathy for my ex-partner's vulnerability.

More recently, the dynamics of abuse have touched close to home as we all struggle to understand the events of September 11, 2001. Each person thinks of that day differently. My family, for example, has endured our evolving experience of living a few blocks from the World Trade Center site. Others, more distant from the site or the event, are unaware of its long-term effect.

In a recent poll conducted by the New York Post, 47 percent of New Yorkers want the towers rebuilt. Bill Pullman, the actor, took this sentiment one step further by saying, "Something should be built that has a larger emphasis than the Twin Towers."[39] That reaction is exactly the sentiment that prevents us from learning something from the violence to which we are exposed. We should learn from that violence and respond by changing, instead of by rebuilding the same or something larger. We should learn more about the triggers that may cause violence toward us, and think more critically about how we treat and/or relate to the people who react so violently against us.

One artist's rendering of a new World Trade Center suggests the kind of self-reflection I seek.[40] The artist offers digging down as a path to healing. He suggests two holes the exact size and shape of the towers, placed below ground. As is clear from the examples of countertransference and projection provided here, looking down into the depths of the violence in our own lives, is the path toward recovery not only for ourselves but also if we hope to help others.

Mandatory policies that seek in effect to eradicate intimate violence as if it were the exclusive property of male aggression can take us only so far. Externalizing violence, projecting aggression onto others, and refusing to take responsibility for its role in violent dynamics are all forms of turning away from, rather than attending to, intimate abuse. I started this book with a story of a mother hitting her young son—and the son striking back. I want to end with that image because it so dramatically portrays the dynamic of intimate abuse. Violence is endemic to the intimate relationship and therefore offers each of us an opportunity to acknowledge it, make choices about it, and develop new forms of relating with loved ones. It is because intimate violence is so close to home that we may just have a chance to work some of it through.

Notes

Prologue

1. Mieko Yoshihama and Linda G. Mills, "When is the Personal Professional in Public Child Welfare Practice? The Influence of Intimate Partner and Child Abuse Histories on Workers in Domestic Violence Cases," *Child Abuse and Neglect: The International Journal* 27 (2003): 319–336.

2. Lonnie H. Athens, *The Creation of Dangerous Violent Criminals* (Urbana: University of Illinois Press, 1992), 46–56.

3. Murray A. Straus, Richard J. Gelles, and Suzanne K. Steinmetz, *Behind Closed Doors: Violence in the American Family* (Garden City, N.Y.: Anchor Press, 1980), 100.

4. Ibid.

5. See, for example, Susan Schechter, *Women and Male Violence: The Visions and Struggles of the Battered Women's Movement* (Boston: South End Press, 1982), 216–24.

6. Sayantani Dasgupta and Shamita das Dasgupta, "Journeys: Reclaiming South Asian Feminism," in *Our Feet Walk the Sky: Women of the South Asian Diaspora*, ed. Women of South Asian Descent Collective (San Francisco: Aunt Lute Books, 1993), 123–30. See also Michelle S. Jacobs's introduction to *Feminist Legal Theory: An Antiessentialist Reader*, ed. Nancy E. Dowd and Michelle S. Jacobs (New York: New York University Press, 2003), 1–3; and Anannya Bhattacharjee, "Whose Safety? Women of Color and the Violence of Law Enforcement," Justice Visions working paper (Philadelphia: American Friends Service Committee, 2001).

7. See, for example, Sally L. Satel, "It's Always His Fault," *Women's Quarterly* Independent Women's Forum, summer 1997, at http://www.iwf.org/pubs/twq/su97a.shtml

8. Richard A. Berk, Alec Campbell, Ruth Klap, and Bruce Western, "A Bayesian Analysis of the Colorado Springs Spouse Abuse Experiment," *Journal of Criminal Law and Criminology* 83 (1992): 170–200.

9. Lawrence W. Sherman, Janell D. Schmidt, Dennis P. Rogan, Douglas A. Smith, Patrick R. Gartin, Ellen G. Cohn, Dean J. Collins, and Anthony R. Bacich, "The Variable Effects of Arrest on Criminal Careers: The Milwaukee Domestic Violence Experiment," *Journal of Criminal Law and Criminology* 83 (1992): 137–69.

10. Robert C. Davis, Barbara E. Smith, and Laura Nickles, "The Deterrent Effect of Prosecuting Domestic Violence Misdemeanors," *Crime and Delinquency* 44 (1998): 441.

11. Michael P. Johnson, "Patriarchal Terrorism and Common Couple Violence: Two Forms of Violence Against Women," *Journal of Marriage and the Family* 57 (1995): 283–94.

12. See Lewis Okun, "Termination or Resumption of Cohabitation in Woman Battering Relationships: A Statistical Study," in *Coping with Family Violence: Research and Policy Perspectives*, ed. Gerald T. Hotaling, David Finkelhor, John T. Kirkpatrick, and Murray A. Straus (Beverly Hills, Calif.: Sage, 1988); Sascha Griffing, Deborah F. Ragin, Robert E. Sage, Lorraine Madry, Lewis E. Bingham, and Beny J. Primm, "Domestic Violence Survivors' Self-Identified Reasons for Returning to Abusive Relationships," *Journal of Interpersonal Violence* 17 (2002): 306–19.

13. See A. Jay McKeel and Michael J. Sporakowski, "How Shelter Counselors' Views about Responsibility for Wife Abuse Relate to Services They Provide to Battered Women," *Journal of Family Violence* 8 (1993): 101–12.

14. Sherman, et al., "The Variable Effects of Arrest," 160.

15. For further discussion on why women stay, see research outlined in chapter 3, "Why Women Stay." For further discussion on the dynamic of intimate abuse, see chapter 5.

16. For further discussion of lesbian intimate violence, see chapter 4.

17. Murray A. Straus, "The Controversy over Domestic Violence by Women: A Methodological, Theoretical, and Sociology of Science Analysis," in *Violence in Intimate Relationships*, ed. Ximena B. Arriaga and Stuart Oskamp (Thousand Oaks, Calif.: Sage, 1999), 17–44.

18. For further discussion on research regarding women's aggression, see chapter 4. See chapter 5 for a discussion on the dynamic of intimate abuse.

19. Douglas K. Snyder and Nancy S. Scheer, "Predicting Disposition Following Brief Residence at a Shelter for Battered Women," *American Journal of Community Psychology* 9 (1981): 559–65.

20. Griffing et al., "Domestic Violence Survivors' Self-Identified Reasons," 313–16.

21. Einat Peled, Zvi Eisikovits, Guy Enosh, and Zeev Winstock, "Choice and Empowerment for Battered Women Who Stay: Toward a Constructivist Model," *Social Work* 45 (2000): 9–25.

22. Lawrence W. Sherman and Richard A. Berk, "The Minneapolis Domestic Violence Experiment," *Police Foundation Reports*, April 1984, 67.

23. Ibid.; Raymond Paternoster, Robert Brame, Ronet Bachman, and Lawrence W. Sherman, "Do Fair Procedures Matter? The Effect of Procedural Justice on Spouse Assault," *Law and Society Review* 31 (1997): 163–204.

24. For a brief review of studies on such negative effects, see Anne Atkins, "Why Abortion Is Bad for Your Mental Health," *Daily Telegraph*, July 3, 2002, 23.

25. Sue Clough, "Snooker Star Cleared of Rape 'Is Real Victim,'" *Daily Telegraph*, July 3, 2002, 3.

26. Alan Travis, "Clinic for Child Abusers Forced to Close," *Guardian*, July 5, 2002, 9.

CHAPTER ONE
The Ground Zero of Intimate Abuse

1. Fran H. Norris, "50,000 Disaster Victims Speak: An Empirical Review of Empirical Literature, 1981–2001, Executive Summary" (Washington, D.C.: National Center for PTSD, Center for Mental Health Services, 2001), 11–12.

2. Judith Herman, *Trauma and Recovery: The Aftermath of Violenc—From Domestic Abuse to Political Terror* (New York: Basic Books, 1997), 159–60.

3. Susan J. Brison, *Aftermath: Violence and the Remaking of a Self* (Princeton, N.J.: Princeton University Press, 2002), 39–40.

4. Norris, "50,000 Disaster Victims Speak," 7.

5. I have changed the child's name to protect the family's identity.

6. Herman, *Trauma and Recovery*, 175–95.

7. Monte Morin, "Jim Brown's Wife Testifies That She Lied about Abuse," *Los Angeles Times*, September 2, 1999, B1.

8. Monte Morin, "Jury to Begin Weighing Jim Brown Threat Case," *Los Angeles Times*, September 9, 1999, B3.

9. Donald J. Rebovich, "Prosecution Response to Domestic Violence: Results of a Survey of Large Jurisdictions," in *Do Arrests and Restraining Orders Work?* ed. Eve S. Buzawa and Carl G. Buzawa (Thousand Oaks, Calif.: Sage, 1996), 176–91.

10. Nancy Kathleen Sugg and Thomas Inui, "Primary Care Physicians' Response to Domestic Violence: Opening Pandora's Box," *Journal of the American Medical Association* 267 (1992): 3157–60.

11. For an elaboration of this point, see Linda G. Mills, "Killing Her Softly: Intimate Abuse and the Violence of State Intervention," *Harvard Law Review* 113 (1999): 550–613.

12. Monte Morin, "Brown Guilty of Vandalism, but Is Cleared of Threats," *Los Angeles Times*, September 11, 1999, B1.

13. Morin, "Jim Brown's Wife Testifies."

14. For one of the early examples of this line of reasoning, see Susan Schechter, *Women and Male Violence: The Visions and Struggles of the Battered Women's Movement* (Boston: South End Press, 1982), 216–24.

15. Ibid., 232–34.

16. Ibid., 25–27.

17. Phyllis Goldfarb, "Describing without Circumscribing: Questioning the Construction of Gender in the Discourse of Intimate Violence," *George Washington Law Review* 64 (1996): 582–631.

18. See, for example, work contained in *Of Mice and Women: Aspects of Female Aggression*, ed. Kaj Björkqvist and Pirkko Niemelä (New York: Academic Press, 1992).

19. L. Kevin Hamberger and Theresa Potente, "Counseling Heterosexual Women Arrested for Domestic Violence: Implications for Theory and Practice," *Violence and Victims* 9 (1994): 127.

20. See discussion of the following study in chapter 4: Felicity A. Goodyear-Smith and Tannis M. Laidlaw, "Aggressive Acts and Assaults in Intimate Relationships: Toward an Understanding of the Literature," *Behavioral Sciences and the Law* 17 (1999): 290–91.

21. R. Emerson Dobash and Russell P. Dobash, "Violent Men and Violent Contexts," in *Rethinking Violence against Women*, ed. R. Emerson Dobash and Russell P. Dobash (Thousand Oaks, Calif.: Sage, 1998), 141–68.

22. Murray A. Straus, Richard J. Gelles, and Suzanne K. Steinmetz, *Behind Closed Doors: Violence in the American Family* (Garden City, N.Y.: Anchor Press, 1980), 100.

23. Donald G. Dutton, *The Domestic Assault of Women: Psychological and Criminal Justice Perspectives* (Vancouver: University of British Columbia Press, 1995), 66.

24. Martha Mahoney, "Legal Images of Battered Women: Redefining the Issue of Separation," *Michigan Law Review* 90 (1991): 61–63.

25. See discussion of the following study in chapter 2: Lawrence W. Sherman, Janell D. Schmidt, Dennis P. Rogan, Douglas A. Smith, Patrick R. Gartin, Ellen G. Cohn, Dean J. Collins, and Anthony R. Bacich, "The Variable Effects of Arrest on Criminal Careers: The Milwaukee Domestic Violence Experiment," *Journal of Criminal Law and Criminology* 83 (1992): 160.

26. Anannya Bhattacharjee, "Whose Safety? Women of Color and the Violence of Law Enforcement," Justice Visions working paper (Philadelphia: American Friends Service Committee, 2001), 26.

CHAPTER TWO
Mandatory Policies as Crime Reduction Strategies

1. Bernadette Dunn Sewell, Note, "History of Abuse: Societal, Judicial, and Legislative Responses to the Problem of Wife Beating," *Suffolk University Law Review* 23 (1989): 994–96.

2. Sylvia I. Mignon and William M. Holmes, "Police Response to Mandatory Arrest Laws," *Crime and Delinquency* 41 (1995): 434–35.

3. Patt Morrison, "In Foundation, a First Act Tragedy and Second Act Farce," *Los Angeles Times*, November 5, 1999, B1.

4. For a history of these policies, see Jeffrey Fagan, "The Criminalization of Domestic Violence: Promises and Limits," Department of Justice, National Institute of Justice Research Report (Washington, D.C. 1996): 6–10; Alisa Smith, "Domestic Violence Laws: The Voices of Battered Women," *Violence and Victims* 16 (2001): 91–92.

5. See, for example, Evan Stark, "Mandatory Arrest of Batterers: A Reply to Its Critics," in *Do Arrests and Restraining Orders Work?* ed. Eve S. Buzawa and Carl G. Buzawa (Thousand Oaks, Calif.: Sage, 1996), 127–28.

6. Studies have shown that police make fewer arrests in domestic assaults than in stranger assaults. See Eve S. Buzawa, Thomas L. Austin, and Carl G. Buzawa, "Responding to Crimes of Violence against Women: Gender Differences versus Organizational Imperatives," *Crime and Delinquency* 41 (1995): 460.

7. In terms of child abuse and medical reporting, class and race have been shown to affect the rates at which these professionals report. See Robert L. Hampton and Eli H. Newberger, "Child Abuse Incidence and Reporting by Hospitals: Significance of Severity, Class, and Race," in *Coping with Family Violence: Research and Policy Perspec-*

tives, ed. Gerald T. Hotaling, David Finkelhor, John T. Kirkpatrick, and Murray A. Straus (Thousand Oaks, Calif.: Sage, 1988), 212–21. Machaela Hoctor argues that the potential discrimination associated with a mandatory arrest scheme can be overcome with proper training. Machaela M. Hoctor, "Domestic Violence as a Crime against the State: The Need for Mandatory Arrest in California," *California Law Review* 85 (1997): 701–47.

8. Joan Zorza and Laurie Woods, "Mandatory Arrest: Problems and Possibilities," National Battered Women's Law Project, National Center on Women and Family Law, (1994).

9. See Cheryl Hanna, "No Right to Choose: Mandated Victim Participation in Domestic Violence Prosecutions," *Harvard Law Review* 109 (1996): 1877–78, 1886; Hoctor, "Domestic Violence as a Crime against the State," 653–55.

10. See, generally, Linda G. Mills, "Killing Her Softly: Intimate Abuse and the Violence of State Intervention," *Harvard Law Review* 113 (1999): 550–613.

11. See essays contained in *Feminist Legal Theory: An Anti-essentialist Reader,* ed. Nancy E. Dowd and Michelle S. Jacobs (New York: New York University Press, 2003).

12. Lawrence W. Sherman and Richard A. Berk, "The Specific Deterrent Effects of Arrest for Domestic Assault," *American Sociological Review* 49 (1984): 261–72.

13. The other five published studies are presented in Richard A. Berk, Alec Campbell, Ruth Klap, and Bruce Western, "A Bayesian Analysis of the Colorado Springs Spouse Abuse Experiment," *Journal of Criminal Law and Criminology* 83 (1992): 170–200; Franklyn W. Dunford, David Huizinga, and Delbert S. Elliott, "The Role of Arrest in Domestic Assault: The Omaha Police Experiment," *Criminology* 28 (1990): 183–206; J. David Hirschel and Ira W. Hutchison III, "Female Spouse Abuse and the Police Response: The Charlotte, North Carolina, Experiment," *Journal of Criminal Law and Criminology* 83 (1992): 73–119; Antony M. Pate and Edwin E. Hamilton, "Formal and Informal Deterrents to Domestic Violence: The Dade County Spouse Assault Experiment," *American Sociological Review* 57 (1992): 691–97; Lawrence W. Sherman, Janell D. Schmidt, Dennis P. Rogan, Douglas A. Smith, Patrick R. Gartin, Ellen G. Cohn, Dean J. Collins, and Anthony R. Bacich, "The Variable Effects of Arrest on Criminal Careers: The Milwaukee Domestic Violence Experiment," *Journal of Criminal Law and Criminology* 83 (1992): 137–69. The National Institute of Justice funded a study in Atlanta, Georgia, but no results have been published.

14. "Attorney General's Task Force on Family Violence, Final Report," Office of the Attorney General, Department of Justice (Washington, D.C., 1984), 22–25.

15. Arnold Binder and James W. Meeker, "Experiments as Reforms," *Journal of Criminal Justice* 16 (1988): 348.

16. *Sorichetti v. City of New York,* 482 N.E. 2d 70 (N.Y. 1985).

17. *Thurman v. City of Torrington,* 595 F.Supp. 1521 (D. Conn. 1984). For a detailed description of the case, see Eve S. Buzawa and Carl G. Buzawa, *Domestic Violence: The Criminal Justice Response* (Westport, Conn.: Auburn House, 1992), 102–3.

18. Public Health and Welfare Justice System Improvement Act, 42 UCS §3796hh, 1994.

19. For a chart outlining policies in various jurisdictions, see Bonnie Brandl and Tess Meuer, "Domestic Abuse in Later Life," *Elder Law Journal* 8 (2000): 323–35.

20. Stark, "Mandatory Arrest of Batterers."

21. Sherman et al., "The Variable Effects of Arrest on Criminal Careers."

22. Callie Marie Rennison and Sarah Welchans, "Intimate Partner Violence," Bureau of Justsice Statistics Special Report, Department of Justice (Washington, D.C., 2000).

23. Smith, "Domestic Violence Laws," 11, 102.

24. Kimberlé Crenshaw, "Mapping the Margins: Intersectionality, Identity Politics, and Violence against Women of Color," *Stanford Law Review* 43 (1991): 1257.

25. Franklyn W. Dunford, "The Measurement of Recidivism in Cases of Spousal Assault," *Journal of Criminal Law and Criminology* 83 (1992): 122–23.

26. Hirschel and Hutchison, "Female Spouse Abuse and the Police Response."

27. Berk et al., "A Bayesian Analysis," 198.

28. Pate and Hamilton, "Formal and Informal Deterrents to Domestic Violence," 691.

29. Berk et al., "A Bayesian Analysis," 198.

30. Ibid., 199.

31. Sherman et al., "The Variable Effects of Arrest on Criminal Careers."

32. Lawrence W. Sherman, Janell D. Schmidt, and Dennis P. Rogan, *Policing Domestic Violence: Experiments and Dilemmas* (New York: Free Press, 1992), 256–57.

33. See David A. Ford and Mary Jean Regoli, "The Preventive Impacts of Policies for Prosecuting Wife Batterers," in *Domestic Violence: The Changing Criminal Justice Response*, ed. Eve S. Buzawa and Carl G. Buzawa (Westport, Conn.: Auburn House, 1992), 181, 182–83.

34. Donald J. Rebovich, "Prosecution Response to Domestic Violence: Results of a Survey of Large Jurisdictions," in *Do Arrests and Restraining Orders Work?* ed. Eve S. Buzawa and Carl G. Buzawa (Thousand Oaks, Calif.: Sage, 1996): 176–91.

35. Casey G. Gwinn and Anne O'Dell, "Stopping the Violence: The Role of the Police Officer and the Prosecutor," *Western State University Law Review* 20 (1993): 1506.

36. Rebovich, "Prosecution Response to Domestic Violence," 182–83.

37. Ibid., 183.

38. Ibid., 183, 186.

39. Sarah Kershaw, "Digital Photos Give the Police a New Edge in Abuse Cases," *New York Times*, September 3, 2002, A1.

40. See David A. Ford and Mary Jean Regoli, "The Criminal Prosecution of Wife Assaulters: Process, Problems, and Effects," in *Legal Responses to Wife Assault: Current Trends and Evaluation*, ed. N. Zoe Hilton (Newbury Park, Calif.: Sage, 1993), 157–58.

41. Lawrence W. Sherman and Richard A. Berk, "The Minneapolis Domestic Violence Experiment," *Police Foundation Reports*, April 1984, 6–7.

42. Eve S. Buzawa, Thomas L. Austin, James Bannon, and James Jackson, "Role of Victim Preference in Determining Police Response to Victims of Domestic Violence," in *Domestic Violence: The Changing Criminal Justice Response*, ed. Eve S. Buzawa and Carl G. Buzawa (Wesport, Conn.: Auburn House, 1992), 262, 265.

43. Robert C. Davis, Barbara E. Smith, and Laura B. Nickles, "The Deterrent Effect of Prosecuting Domestic Violence Misdemeanors," *Crime and Delinquency* 44 (1998): 441.

44. Judith McFarlane, Pam Willson, Dorothy Lemmey, and Ann Malecha, "Women Filing Assault Charges on an Intimate Partner: Criminal Justice Outcome and Future Violence Experienced," *Violence Against Women* 6 (2000): 404.

45. Linda G. Mills, *The Heart of Intimate Abuse: New Interventions in Child Welfare, Criminal Justice and Healthcare Settings* (New York: Springer, 1998), 86–87.

46. Martha L. Coulter and Ronald A. Chez, "Domestic Violence Victims Support Mandatory Reporting: For Others," *Journal of Family Violence* 12 (1997): 354–55.

47. Alisa Smith, "It's My Decision Isn't It?" *Violence Against Women* 6 (2000): 1395, 1398.

48. Winifred Yu, "Doctors Urged to Be on Lookout for Victims of Domestic Violence," Albany (N.Y.) *Times Union*, March 5, 1997, B5.

49. Evan Stark and Anne Flitcraft, "Violence among Intimates: An Epidemiological Review," in *Handbook of Family Violence*, ed. Vincent Van Hasselt, Randall Morrison, Alan Bellack, and Michel Herson (New York: Plenum Press, 1988), 302.

50. Elaine H. Carmen, Patricia P. Reiker, and Trudy Mills, "Victims of Violence and Psychiatric Illness," *American Journal of Psychiatry* 141 (1984): 378–83.

51. Stark and Flitcraft, "Violence among Intimates," 304.

52. Murray A. Straus and Christine Smith, "Family Patterns and Primary Prevention of Family Violence," in *Physical Violence in American Families: Risk Factors and Adaptations to Violence in 8,145 Families*, ed. Murray A. Straus and Richard J. Gelles (New Brunswick, N.J.: Transaction, 1995), 510.

53. Ola W. Barnett and Ronald W. Fagan, "Alcohol Use in Male Spouse Abusers and Their Female Partners," *Journal of Family Violence* 8 (1993): 19.

54. Stark and Flitcraft, "Violence among Intimates," 301.

55. Michael R. Rand, "Violence-Related Injuries Treated in Hospital Emergency Departments," Department of Justice Statistics (Washington, D.C. 1997).

56. Commonwealth Fund, Commission on Women's Health, "First Comprehensive National Health Survey of American Women Finds Them at Significant Risk," press release, Washington, D.C., July 14, 1993.

57. Laura E. Lund, "What Happens When Health Practitioners Report Domestic Violence Injuries to the Police? A Study of the Law Enforcement Response to Injury Reports," *Violence and Victims* 14 (1999): 210.

58. Judith McFarlane, Barbara Parker, and Karen Soeken, "Abuse during Pregnancy: Frequency, Severity, Perpetrator, and Risk Factors of Homicide," *Public Health Nursing* 12 (1995): 284–89.

59. Linda R. Chambliss, R. Curtis Bay, and Richard F. Jones III, "Domestic Violence: An Educational Imperative?," *American Journal of Obstetrics and Gynecology* 172 (1995): 1035–38.

60. Nancy Kathleen Sugg and Thomas Inui, "Primary Care Physicians' Response to Domestic Violence: Opening Pandora's Box," *Journal of the American Medical Association* 267 (1992): 3157–60.

61. See, for example, Ariella Hyman, Dean Schillinger, and Bernard Lo, "Laws Mandating Reporting of Domestic Violence: Do They Promote Patient Well-Being?" *Journal of the American Medical Association* 273 (1995): 1781–87.

62. See essays contained in Dowd and Jacobs, *Feminist Legal Theory*.

63. Donna Wills, "Domestic Violence: The Case for Aggressive Prosecution," *UCLA Women's Law Journal* 7 (1997): 173–82.

64. Gwinn and O'Dell, "Stopping the Violence."

65. Yael Danieli, "Confronting the Unimaginable: Psychotherapists' Reactions to Victims of the Nazi Holocaust," in *Human Adaptation to Extreme Stress: From the Holocaust to Vietnam*, ed. John P. Wilson, Zev Harel, and Boaz Kahana (New York: Plenum Press, 1988), 221.

66. Robert Spagnoletti, remarks at the First Annual Gender, Sexuality, and the Law Symposium (Washington, D.C., Georgetown University Law Center on Violence and State Accountability Conference, February 20–21, 1998), 4, 5.

67. Ibid.

68. Rebovich, "Prosecution Response to Domestic Violence."

69. Sandra L. Bloom, "The Germ Theory of Trauma: The Impossibility of Ethical Neutrality," in *Secondary Traumatic Stress: Self-Care Issues for Clinicians, Researchers, and Educators*, ed. B. Hudnall Stamm (Lutherville, Md.: Sidran Press, 1999), 257–76.

70. John M. Dorsey, "Forensic Psychiatry of Schizophrenia in Survivors," in *Massive Psychic Trauma*, ed. Henry Krystal (New York: International Universities Press, 1968), 142.

CHAPTER THREE
Power over Women in Abusive Relationships

1. Emanuel Tanay, "Initiation of Psychotherapy with Survivors of Nazi Persecution," in *Massive Psychic Trauma*, ed. Henry Krystal (New York: International Universities Press, 1968), 225.

2. Judith Herman, *Trauma and Recovery* (New York: Basic Books, 1997), 139.

3. Tanay, "Initiation of Psychotherapy," 225.

4. See Carl G. Jung, *The Practice of Psychotherapy: Essays on the Psychology of the Transference and other Subjects*, 2d ed., tran. R. F. C. Hull, ed. Herbert Read, Michael Fordham, and Gerhard Adler (New York: Pantheon, 1966), 164–67.

5. Yael Danieli, "Confronting the Unimaginable: Psychotherapists' Reactions to Victims of the Nazi Holocaust," in *Human Adaptation to Extreme Stress: From the Holocaust to Vietnam*, ed. John P. Wilson, Zev Harel, and Boaz Kahana (New York: Plenum Press, 1988), 219–21, 226–29.

6. Ibid., 221–26.

7. John M. Dorsey, "Forensic Psychiatry of Schizophrenia in Survivors," in *Massive Psychic Trauma*, ed. Henry Krystal (New York: International Universities Press, 1968), 142.

8. Danieli, "Confronting the Unimaginable," 226.

9. Ibid.

10. Ibid., 227.

11. Ibid.

12. Some researchers have characterized this rage as the stress associated with treating a trauma victim. See Tanay, "Initiation of Psychotherapy," 224.

13. Danieli, "Confronting the Unimaginable," 229.

14. Ibid., 231.

15. Ibid., 231–32.

16. Ibid., 235.

17. Ibid., 228.

18. See, for example, Ola W. Barnett and Alyce D. LaViolette, *It Could Happen to Anyone: Why Battered Women Stay* (Newbury Park, Calif.: Sage, 1993), 93–116.

19. Lenore E. Walker, *The Battered Woman* (New York: Harper and Row, 1979), 42–54.

20. Lenore E. Walker, *The Battered Woman Syndrome* (New York: Springer, 1984), 126–38.

21. Herman, *Trauma and Recovery*, 1–4.

22. Ibid., 115–29.

23. Ibid.

24. Donald G. Dutton, *The Domestic Assault of Women: Psychological and Criminal Justice Perspectives* (Vancouver: University of British Columbia Press, 1995), 190.

25. For a discussion of these concepts, see ibid., 190–95.

26. Lewis Okun, "Termination or Resumption of Cohabitation in Woman Battering Relationships: A Statistical Study," in *Coping with Family Violence: Research and Policy Perspectives*, ed. Gerald T. Hotaling, David Finkelhor, John T. Kirkpatrick, and Murray A. Straus (Beverly Hills, Calif.: Sage, 1988), 112–13.

27. Douglas K. Snyder and Nancy S. Scheer, "Predicting Disposition Following Brief Residence at a Shelter for Battered Women," *American Journal of Community Psychology* 9 (1981): 559–65.

28. For an illustration of such an argument, see Carol Gilligan, *In a Different Voice: Psychological Theory and Women's Development* (Cambridge, Mass.: Harvard University Press, 1982), 39–45. See also, Sascha Griffing, Deborah F. Ragin, Robert E. Sage, Lorraine Madry, Lewis E. Bingham, and Beny J. Primm, "Domestic Violence Survivors' Self-Identified Reasons for Returning to Abusive Relationships," *Journal of Interpersonal Violence* 17 (2002): 306–19.

29. Zvi Eisikovits, and Eli Buchbinder, *Locked in a Violent Embrace: Understanding and Intervening in Domestic Violence* (Thousand Oaks, Calif.: Sage, 2000), 29–42.

30. Jody Brown, "Working toward Freedom from Violence: The Process of Change in Battered Women," *Violence Against Women* 3 (1997): 5–26.

31. Linda G. Mills, *The Heart of Intimate Abuse: New Interventions in Child Welfare: Criminal Justice and Health Care Settings* (New York: Springer, 1998), 36–37.

32. See, for example, Shamita das Dasgupta and Sujata Warrier, "In the Footsteps of 'Arundhati': Asian Indian Women's Experience of Domestic Violence in the United States," *Violence Against Women* 2 (1996): 252. See also Beverly Horsburgh, "Lifting the Veil of Secrecy: Domestic Violence in the Jewish Community," *Harvard Women's Law Journal* 18 (1995): 171–217.

33. Leti Volpp, "Feminism versus Multiculturalism," *Columbia Law Review* 101 (2001): 1181–1218.

34. See, for example, Mieko Yoshihama, "Reinterpreting Strength and Safety in a Socio-Cultural Context: Dynamics of Domestic Violence and Experiences of Women of Japanese Descent," *Children and Youth Services Review* 22 (2000): 207–9.

35. Volpp, "Feminism versus Multiculturalism;" Virginia Goldner, "Morality and Multiplicity: Perspectives on the Treatment of Violence in Intimate Life," *Journal of Marital and Family Therapy* 25 (1999): 325–36; Kimberlé Crenshaw, "Mapping the Margins: Intersectionality, Identity Politics, and Violence against Women of Color," *Stanford Law Review* 43 (1991): 1241–99.

36. Horsburgh, "Lifting the Veil of Secrecy."

37. "Revolutions within Communities: Issues in Representing Immigrant Victims," *Fordham Urban Law Journal* 29 (2001): 70–119.

38. Gwat-yong Lie, Rebecca Schilit, Judy Bush, Marilyn Montagne, and Lynn Reyes, "Lesbians in Currently Aggressive Relationships: How Frequently Do They Report Aggressive Past Relationships?" *Violence and Victims* 6 (1991): 121–35.

39. For example, see Donna Wills, "Domestic Violence: The Case for Aggressive Prosecution," *UCLA Women's Law Journal* 7 (1997): 173–82.

40. See Crenshaw, "Mapping the Margins"; Jane Flax, *Thinking Fragments: Psychoanalysis, Feminism and Postmodernism in the Contemporary West* (Berkeley and Los Angeles: University of California Press, 1990).

41. See Kathleen Neal Cleaver, "Racism, Civil Rights, and Feminism," and Angela P. Harris, "Race and Essentialism in Feminist Legal Theory," both in *Critical Race Feminism*, ed. Adrien K. Wing (New York: New York University Press, 1997), 11–18, 35–43.

42. I argue this point in my earlier work. See, for example, Linda G. Mills, "Feminist Phallacies: The Politics of Prenatal Drug Exposure and the Power of Law," *Law and Social Inquiry* 25 (2000): 1215–26.

43. Vikki Bell, *Interrogating Incest: Feminism, Foucault and the Law* (London: Routledge, 1993).

44. Mills, "Feminist Phallacies."

45. Michel Foucault, *The History of Sexuality: An Introduction, Volume One* (New York: Vintage Books, 1990), 99.

46. Melanie L. O'Neill and Patricia K. Kerig, "Attributions of Self-Blame and Perceived Control as Moderators of Adjustment in Battered Women," *Journal of Interpersonal Violence* 15 (2000): 1037.

47. Ibid., 1044.

48. Tracy Bennett Herbert, Roxane Cohen Silver, and John H. Ellard, "Coping with an Abusive Relationship: How and Why Do Women Stay?" *Journal of Marriage and the Family* 53 (1991): 311–25.

CHAPTER FOUR
Are Women as Aggressive as Men?

1. See John Johnson, "A New Side to Domestic Violence: Arrests of Women Have Risen Sharply since Passage of Tougher Laws," *Los Angeles Times*, April 27, 1996, A1.

2. See, for example, Marion Wanless, "Mandatory Arrest: A Step toward Eradicating Domestic Violence, But Is It Enough?" *University of Illinois Law Review* (1996): 533–86.

3. Kaj Björkqvist and Pirkko Niemelä, "New Trends in the Study of Female Aggression," in *Of Mice and Women: Aspects of Female Aggression*, ed. Kaj Björkqvist and Pirkko Niemelä (New York: Academic Press, 1992), 4.

4. Arnold H. Buss, *The Psychology of Aggression* (New York: Wiley, 1961), 1–16; Seymour Feshbach, "The Function of Aggression and the Regulation of Aggressive Drive," *Psychological Review*, 71 (1964): 257–72; Björkqvist and Niemelä, "New Trends," 4.

5. For this emerging theme, see Linda G. Mills, "Killing Her Softly: Intimate Abuse and the Violence of State Intervention," *Harvard Law Review* 113 (1999): 550–613.

6. Lynn Magdol, Terrie E. Moffitt, Avshalom Caspi, Denise L. Newman, Jeffrey Fagan, and Phil A. Silva, "Gender Differences in Partner Violence in a Birth Cohort of 21-Year-Olds: Bridging the Gap between Clinical and Epidemiological Approaches," *Journal of Consulting and Clinical Psychology* 65 (1997): 68–78.

7. Ibid.

8. Ibid.

9. John Langley, Judy Martin, and Shyamala Nada–Raja, "Physical Assault among 21-Year Olds by Partners," *Journal of Interpersonal Violence* 12 (1997): 675–84.

10. Murray A. Straus and Richard J. Gelles, "Societal Change and Change in Family Violence from 1975 to 1985 as Revealed by Two National Surveys," *Journal of Marriage and the Family* 48 (1986): 470–71.

11. Robert E. Billingham and Alan R. Sack, "Conflict Tactics and the Level of Emotional Commitment among Unmarrieds," *Human Relations* 40 (1987): 69.

12. Murray A. Straus, "The Controversy over Domestic Violence by Women: A Methodological, Theoretical, and Sociology of Science Analysis," in *Violence in Intimate Relationships*, ed. Ximena B. Arriaga and Stuart Oskamp (Thousand Oaks, Calif.: Sage, 1999), 19.

13. Jacquelyn W. White and Mary P. Koss, "Courtship Violence: Incidence in a National Sample of Higher Education Students," *Violence and Victims* 6 (1991): 247–56.

14. David R. Jezl, Christian E. Molidor, and Tracy L. Wright, "Physical, Sexual and Psychological Abuse in High School Dating Relationships: Prevalence Rates and Self-Esteem Issues," *Child and Adolescent Social Work Journal* 13 (1996): 69–87.

15. Robert L. Bowman and Holly M. Morgan, "A Comparison of Rates of Verbal and Physical Abuse on Campus by Gender and Sexual Orientation," *College Student Journal* 32 (1998): 43–52.

16. Lettie L. Lockhart, Barbara W. White, Vicki Causby, and Alicia Isaac, "Letting Out the Secret: Violence in Lesbian Relationships," *Journal of Interpersonal Violence* 9 (1994): 469–92.

17. Gwat-yong Lie and Sabrina Gentlewarrier, "Intimate Violence in Lesbian Relationships: Discussion of Survey Findings and Practice Implications," *Journal of Social Service Research* 15 (1991): 41–59.

18. Ronald P. Rohner, "Sex Differences in Aggression: Phylogenetic and Enculturation Perspectives," *Ethos* 4 (1976): 57–72.

19. Victoria K. Burbank, "Female Aggression in Cross-Cultural Perspective," *Behavior Science Research* 21 (1987): 70–100.

20. Alan W. Leschied, Anne L. Cummings, Michelle Van Brunschot, Alison Cunningham, and Angela Saunders, "Aggression in Adolescent Girls: Implications for Policy, Prevention, and Treatment," *Canadian Psychology* 42 (2001), 200–215; H. B. Kimberly Cook, "Matrifocality and Female Aggression in Margariteño Society," and Douglas P. Fry, "Female Aggression among the Zapotec of Oaxaca, Mexico," all in *Of Mice and Women: Aspects of Female Aggression*, ed. Kaj Björkqvist and Pirkko Niemelä (New York: Academic Press, 1992), 99–106, 144–62, 187–99.

21. Kaj Björkqvist, Kirsti M. J. Lagerspetz, and Ari Kaukiainen, "Do Girls Manipulate and Boys Fight? Developmental Trends in Regard to Direct and Indirect Aggression," *Aggressive Behavior* 18 (1992): 117–27.

22. See Adam Frączek, "Patterns of Aggressive-Hostile Behavior Orientation among Adolescent Boys and Girls," in *Of Mice and Women: Aspects of Female Aggression*, ed. Kaj Björkqvist and Pirkko Niemelä (New York: Academic Press, 1992): 107–12.

23. Björkqvist, Lagerspetz, and Kaukiainen, "Do Girls Manipulate and Boys Fight?"

24. Kaj Björkqvist, "Sex Differences in Physical, Verbal, and Indirect Aggression: A Review of Recent Research," *Sex Roles* 30 (1994): 185.

25. Björkqvist, Lagerspetz, and Kaukiainen, "Do Girls Manipulate and Boys Fight?" 126.

26. Helen Smith and Sandra P. Thomas, "Violent and Nonviolent Girls: Contrasting Perceptions of Anger Experiences, School, and Relationships," *Issues in Mental Health Nursing* 21 (2000): 562.

27. Rolf Kuschel, "'Women Are Women and Men are Men': How Bellonese Women Get Even," in *Of Mice and Women: Aspects of Female Aggression*, ed. Kaj Björkqvist and Pirkko Niemelä (New York: Academic Press, 1992), 183.

28. Burbank, "Female Aggression."

29. Charlene L. Muehlenhard and Stephen W. Cook, "Men's Self-Reports of Unwanted Sexual Activity," *Journal of Sex Research* 24 (1988): 58–72.

30. Phyllis Ellickson, Hilary Saner, and Kimberly A. McGuigan, "Profiles of Violent Youth: Substance Use and Other Concurrent Problems," *American Journal of Public Health* 87 (1997): 985–91.

31. "Crime in the United States 2001," Uniform Crime Reports, Federal Bureau of Investigation, Department of Justice (Washington, D.C., 2002).

32. Richard J. Gelles, *Intimate Violence in Families*, 3d ed. (Thousand Oaks, Calif.: Sage, 1997), 59.

33. Barbara A. Wauchope and Murray A. Straus, "Physical Punishment and Physical Abuse of American Children: Incidence Rates by Age, Gender and Occupational Class," in *Physical Violence in American Families: Risk Factors and Adaptations to Violence in 8,145 Families*, ed. Murray A. Straus and Richard J. Gelles (New Brunswick, N.J.: Transaction, 1995), 135.

34. James A. Fox and Marianne W. Zawitz, "Homicide Trends in the United States," Bureau of Justice Statistics Special Report, Department of Justice (Washington, D.C., November 2002).

35. Donald G. Dutton, *The Domestic Assault of Women: Psychological and Criminal Justice Perspectives* (Vancouver: University of British Columbia Press, 1995), 119.

36. L. Kevin Hamberger and Theresa Potente, "Counseling Heterosexual Women Arrested for Domestic Violence: Implications for Theory and Practice," *Violence and Victims* 9 (1994): 129.

37. Christopher M. Murphy and K. Daniel O'Leary, "Psychological Aggression Predicts Physical Aggression in Early Marriage," *Journal of Consulting and Clinical Psychology* 57 (1989): 582.

38. Ibid., 582.

39. Hamberger and Potente, "Counseling Heterosexual Women."

40. Amy Holtzworth-Munroe, Jeffrey C. Meehan, Katherine Herron, and Gregory L. Stuart, "A Typology of Male Batterers: An Initial Examination," in *Violence in Intimate Relationships*, ed. Ximena B. Arriaga and Stuart Oskamp (Thousand Oaks, Calif.: Sage, 1999), 47–52.

41. Jan E. Stets and Murray A. Straus, "The Marriage License as a Hitting License: A Comparison of Assaults in Dating, Cohabiting, and Married Couples," in *Physical Violence in American Families: Risk Factors and Adaptations to Violence in 8,145 Families*, ed. Murray A. Straus and Richard J. Gelles (New Brunswick, N.J.: Transaction, 1995), 233–35.

42. Jan E. Stets and Murray A. Straus, "Gender Differences in Reporting Marital Violence and its Medical and Psychological Consequences," in *Physical Violence in American Families: Risk Factors and Adaptations to Violence in 8,145 Families*, ed. Murray A. Straus and Richard J. Gelles (New Brunswick, N.J.: Transaction, 1995), 157.

43. Richard A. Berk, Sarah F. Berk, Donileen R. Loseke, and David Rauma, "Mutual Combat and Other Family Violence Myths," in *The Dark Side of Families: Current Family Violence Research*, ed. David Finkelhor, Richard J. Gelles, Gerald T. Hotaling, and Murray A. Straus (Beverly Hills, Calif.: Sage, 1983), 199.

44. See Lisa D. Brush, "Violent Acts and Injurious Outcomes in Married Couples: Methodological Issues in the National Survey of Families and Households," *Gender and Society* 4 (1990): 56–67; Barbara J. Morse, "Beyond the Conflict Tactics Scale: Assessing Gender Differences in Partner Violence," *Violence and Victims* 10 (1995): 251–72.

45. Felicity A. Goodyear–Smith and Tannis M. Laidlaw, "Aggressive Acts and Assaults in Intimate Relationships: Towards an Understanding of the Literature," *Behavioral Sciences and the Law* 17 (1999): 290–91.

46. Ibid.

47. See Diane R. Follingstad, Larry L. Rutledge, Barbara J. Berg, Elizabeth S. Hause, and Darlene S. Polek, "The Role of Emotional Abuse in Physically Abusive Relationships," *Journal of Family Violence* 5 (1990): 108.

48. Murphy and O'Leary, "Psychological Aggression Predicts Physical Aggression in Early Marriage."

49. Follingstad et al., "The Role of Emotional Abuse in Physically Abusive Relationships," 116.

50. See material as discussed in Elizabeth Schneider, *Battered Women and Feminist Lawmaking* (New Haven, Conn.: Yale University Press, 2000), 66, n. 26.

51. Patricia Pearson, *When She Was Bad: How Women Get Away with Murder* (London: Virago Press, 1998), 17–21.

52. Schneider, *Battered Women and Feminist Lawmaking*, 66–67.

53. See Ann Russo, "Lesbians Organizing Lesbians against Battering," in *Same-Sex Domestic Violence: Strategies for Change*, ed. Beth Leventhal and Sandra E. Lundy (Thousand Oaks, Calif.: Sage, 1999), 83–96.

54. Jean LaPlanche and J.-B. Pontalis, *The Language of Psychoanalysis*, trans. Donald Nicholson-Smith (New York: Norton, 1973), 349–56.

55. Mieko Yoshihama and Linda G. Mills, "When is the Personal Professional in Public Child Welfare Practice? The Influence of Intimate Partner and Child Abuse Histories on Workers in Domestic Violence Cases," *Child Abuse and Neglect: The International Journal* 27 (2003): 319–336.

56. Linda G. Mills, *A Penchant for Prejudice: Unraveling Bias in Judicial Decision-making* (Ann Arbor: University of Michigan Press, 1999).

57. Murray A. Straus and Richard J. Gelles, "How Violent Are American Families? Estimates from the National Family Violence Resurvey and Other Studies," and Murray A. Straus, "Ordinary Violence, Child Abuse, and Wife Beating: What Do They Have in Common?" both in *Physical Violence in American Families: Risk Factors and Adaptations to Violence in 8,145 Families*, ed. Murray A. Straus and Richard J. Gelles (New Brunswick, N.J.: Transaction, 1995), 105–6, 407, 410.

58. David Finkelhor, and Jennifer Dziuba-Leatherman, "Victimization of Children," *American Psychologist* 49 (1994): 175.

59. Ibid., 176.

60. Ibid.

CHAPTER FIVE
The Dynamic of Intimate Abuse

1. For an excellent discussion of these issues, see Lonnie H. Athens, "Violentization in Larger Social Context," in *Violent Acts and Violentization: Assessing, Applying, and Developing Lonnie Athens' Theories*, ed. Lonnie H. Athens and Jeffrey T. Ulmer (New York: Elsevier Science Ltd., 2003), 1–7.

2. Sarnoff A. Mednick, Vicki E. Pollock, Jan Volavka, and William F. Gabrielli Jr., "Biology and Violence," in *Criminal Violence*, ed. Marvin E. Wolfgang and Neil Alan Weiner (Beverly Hills, Calif.: Sage, 1982), 21–80.

3. Dorothy Otnow Lewis, *Guilty by Reason of Insanity* (New York: Random House, 1998), 117–20.

4. Lonnie Athens subscribes to a holistic approach, with a focus on environmental influences. See Athens, "Violentization in Larger Social Context."

5. David Finkelhor, and Jennifer Dziuba-Leatherman, "Victimization of Children," *American Psychologist* 49 (1994): 173–83.

6. Ibid.

7. Murray A. Straus, Richard J. Gelles, and Suzanne K. Steinmetz, *Behind Closed Doors: Violence in the American Family*, (Garden City, N.Y.: Anchor Press, 1980), 100.

8. Ibid., 110.

9. Ibid., 114.

10. Lonnie H. Athens, *The Creation of Dangerous Violent Criminals* (Urbana: University of Illinois Press, 1992), 46–56.

11. Donald G. Dutton, *The Domestic Assault of Women: Psychological and Criminal Justice Perspectives* (Vancouver: University of British Columbia Press, 1995).

12. James Gilligan, *Violence: Reflections on a National Epidemic* (New York: Vintage Books, 1996), 103–36.

13. Ibid.

14. Athens, *The Creation of Dangerous Violent Criminals*, 46–56.

15. See *People v. Aris*, 215 Cal.App.3d 1178, 1184, 264 Cal. Rptr. 167, 171 (1989); see also Sandra Stokley, "Woman Inmate Found Suitable for Parole," Riverside (Calif.) *Press-Enterprise*, August 24, 1994, B3.

16. This issue was raised on appeal. The California Court of Appeals found that the judge erred when he prevented Walker from testifying that Brenda Aris suffered from battered woman's syndrome. The court also held that the error was harmless in Brenda's case—that is, even if Walker would have testified that Brenda suffered from the syndrome, the jury still would have convicted her. This is clearly a point of contention. *People v. Aris*, 215 Cal.App.3d 1178, 1201, 264 Cal.Rptr. 167, 180, 182 (1989).

17. Kim Bartholomew, "Avoidance of Intimacy: An Attachment Perspective," *Journal of Social and Personal Relationships* 7 (1990): 147–78.

18. Jamila Bookwala, "The Role of Own and Perceived Partner Attachment in Relationship Aggression," *Journal of Interpersonal Violence* 17 (2002): 84–100.

19. Ibid., 96.

20. Jamila Bookwala and Bozena Zdaniuk, "Adult Attachment Styles and Aggressive Behavior within Dating Relationships," *Journal of Social and Personal Relationships* 15 (1998): 175–90; Nigel Roberts and Patricia Noller, "The Associations between Adult Attachment and Couple Violence: The Role of Communication Patterns and Relationship Satisfaction," in *Attachment Theory and Close Relationships*, ed. Jeffry A. Simpson and W. Steven Rholes (New York: Guilford, 1998), 339.

21. Bookwala, "The Role of Own and Perceived Partner Attachment," 96–97.

22. Ibid., 97.

23. Roberts and Noller, "The Associations between Adult Attachment and Couple Violence," 340.

24. Bookwala, "The Role of Own and Perceived Partner Attachment," 97.

25. Patricia Pearson, *When She Was Bad: How Women Get Away with Murder* (London: Virago Press, 1998).

26. R. Emerson Dobash and Russell P. Dobash, "Violent Men and Violent Contexts," in *Rethinking Violence against Women*, ed. R. Emerson Dobash and Russell P. Dobash (Thousand Oaks, Calif.: Sage, 1998), 153.

27. James Browning and Donald G. Dutton, "Assessment of Wife Assault with the Conflict Tactics Scale: Using Couple Data to Quantify the Differential Reporting Effect," *Journal of Marriage and the Family* 48 (1986): 375–79.

28. Dobash and Dobash, "Violent Men and Violent Contexts," 155.

29. Zvi Eisikovits and Eli Buchbinder, *Locked in a Violent Embrace: Understanding and Intervening in Domestic Violence* (Thousand Oaks, Calif.: Sage, 2000).

30. Ibid., 25.

31. Ibid., 91.

32. Dutton, *The Domestic Assault of Women*, 68.

33. Melanie L. O'Neill and Patricia K. Kerig, "Attributions of Self-Blame and Perceived Control as Moderators of Adjustment in Battered Women," *Journal of Interpersonal Violence* 15 (2000): 1036–49.

34. Murray A. Straus, "The Controversy over Domestic Violence by Women: A Methodological, Theoretical, and Sociology of Science Analysis," in *Violence in Intimate Relationships*, ed. Ximena B. Arriaga and Stuart Oskamp (Thousand Oaks, Calif.: Sage, 1999), 17–44.

35. Christopher M. Murphy and K. Daniel O'Leary, "Psychological Aggression Predicts Physical Aggression in Early Marriage," *Journal of Consulting and Clinical Psychology* 57 (1993): 579–82.

36. Julia C. Babcock, Jennifer Waltz, Neil S. Jacobson, and John M. Gottman, "Power and Violence: The Relation between Communication Patterns, Power Discrepancies, and Domestic Violence," *Journal of Consulting and Clinical Psychology* 61 (1993): 47.

CHAPTER SIX
Changing the System

1. Galla Hendy's story is taken from Deborah Sontag, "Fierce Entanglements," *New York Times Magazine*, November 17, 2002, 56–57.

2. See, for example, Julie Stubbs, "Domestic Violence and Women's Safety: Feminist Challenges to Restorative Justice," in *Restorative Justice and Family Violence*, ed. Heather Strang and John Braithwaite (Cambridge: Cambridge University Press, 2002), 42–61.

3. For a variation on the proposed model, see Lawrence W. Sherman, "Domestic Violence and Restorative Justice: Answering Key Questions," Virginia Journal of Social Policy and Law, 8 (2000): 263–289.

4. For a study that concludes that respect, as well as just procedures, can decrease recidivism, see Raymond Paternoster, Robert Brame, Ronet Bachman, and Lawrence W. Sherman, "Do Fair Procedures Matter? The Effect of Procedural Justice on Spouse Assault," *Law and Society Review* 31 (1997): 163–204.

5. David Ford and Mary Jean Regoli, "The Criminal Prosecution of Wife Assaulters: Process, Problems and Effects," in *Legal Responses to Wife Assault: Current Trends and Evaluation*, ed. N. Zoe Hilton (Newbury Park, Calif.: Sage, 1993), 127–64.

6. "Crime in the United States 2001," Uniform Crime Reports, Federal Bureau of Investigation, Department of Justice (Washington, D.C., 2002).

7. Laura Dugan, Daniel Nagin, and Richard Rosenfeld, "Exposure Reduction or Backlash? The Effects of Domestic Violence Resources on Intimate Partner Homicide," Final Report to the National Institute of Justice (Washington, D.C., 2001), 30, 34.

8. See, for example, W. Vernon Lee and Stephen P. Weinstein, "How Far Have We Come? A Critical Review of the Research on Men Who Batter," in *Alcoholism and Violence: Recent Developments in Alcoholism*, vol. 13, ed. Marc Galanter (New York: Plenum Press, 1997), 337.

9. See Cheryl Hanna, "The Paradox of Hope: The Crime and Punishment of Domestic Violence," *William and Mary Law Review* 39 (1998): 1559–66.

10. Such criteria include age at first offense; stability in residence and employment; family structure and history; support and ties to the community; "past suicide threats or attempts; past threats to kill partners or family members; defendant homicidal or suicidal ideation; history of abuse of weapons, infliction of serious injury on others in prior abusive incidents; the offender's evasiveness and failure to admit specific acts of violence; defendant's access to or ownership of guns; offender history of drug or alcohol abuse; offender's refusal to cooperate with treatment in the past; defendant's statements that he or she cannot live without the partner or beliefs that the partner intends to leave; history of separation violence between the parties; offender's being obsessed or sadistic; offender's feelings of entitlement to or ownership of the battered partner; the victim's assessment of the situation; offender's history of depression or other psychological disorders; offender's history of abusing animals and pets." Randal B. Fritzler and Lenore M. J. Simon, "The Development of a Specialized Domestic Violence Court in Vancouver, Washington Utilizing Innovative Judicial Paradigms," *University of Missouri at Kansas City Law Review* 69 (2000): 164.

11. Betsy Tsai, Note, "The Trend toward Specialized Domestic Violence Courts: Improvements on an Effective Innovation," *Fordham Law Review* 68 (2000): 1292–93.

12. In addition to these commonly mentioned criteria, factors associated with the person's offense and/or arrest might be used. For example, in a study that made use of U.S. Secret Service members' experience at predicting violent behavior, suggestions included strangulation, resisting arrest, violation of protective orders, whether the victim had indicated intent to end the relationship, public acts of violence, and offender's life stressors. See Richard Devine, "Targeting High Risk Domestic Violence Cases: The Cook County, Chicago, Experience," *APR Prosecutor* 34 (2000): 31.

13. Michael P. Johnson, "Patriarchal Terrorism and Common Couple Violence: Two Forms of Violence against Women," *Journal of Marriage and the Family* 57 (1995): 283–94.

14. James Gilligan, *Violence: Reflections on a National Epidemic* (New York: Vintage Books, 1996), 188, 206.

15. John Braithwaite, "Restorative Justice: Assessing Optimistic and Pessimistic Accounts," *Crime and Justice* 25 (1999): 26.

16. Neil S. Jacobson, John M. Gottman, Jennifer Waltz, Regina Rushe, Julia Babcock, and Amy Holtzworth-Munroe, "Affect, Verbal Content, and Psychophysiology in the Arguments of Couples with a Violent Husband," *Journal of Consulting and Clinical Psychology* 62 (1994): 986.

17. See Boyd C. Rollins and Stephen J. Bahr, "A Theory of Power Relationships in Marriage," *Journal of Marriage and the Family* (1976): 619.

18. Donna K. Coker, "Heat of Passion and Wife Killing: Men Who Batter/ Men Who Kill," *Southern California Review of Law and Women's Studies* 2 (1992): 95–99.

19. Ibid., 95–96, citing the narrative of an episode of intimate abuse by the offender: "I thought to myself, 'I'm going to beat the damn truth out of that no-good, rotten bitch.' I started thinking about tying her up and beating her until she talked, but then I thought that if I went that far, she might leave me, so I dropped it. I was scared that if I did do it, then I would end up losing her."

20. Janet A. Johnson, Victoria L. Lutz and Neil Websdale, "Death by Intimacy: Risk Factors for Domestic Violence," *Pace Law Review* 20 (2000): 268.

21. Jacobson et al., "Affect, Verbal Content, and Psychophysiology," 987.

22. Helen S. Pan, Peter H. Neidig, and K. Daniel O'Leary, "Predicting Mild and Severe Husband-to-Wife Physical Aggression," *Journal of Consulting and Clinical Psychology* 62 (1994): 980.

23. Avonne Mason and Virginia Blankenship, "Power and Affiliation Motivation, Stress, and Abuse in Intimate Relationships," *Journal of Personality and Social Psychology* 52 (1987): 209.

24. Jacobson et al., "Affect, Verbal Content, and Psychophysiology," 987.

25. Julia C. Babcock, Jennifer Waltz, Neil S. Jacobson, and John M. Gottman, "Power and Violence: The Relation between Communication Patterns, Power Discrepancies, and Domestic Violence," *Journal of Consulting and Clinical Psychology* 61 (1993): 47.

26. Mason and Blankenship, "Power and Affiliation Motivation," 207.

27. Johnson, Lutz, and Websdale, "Death by Intimacy," 267–68.

28. Jacobson et al., "Affect, Verbal Content, and Psychophysiology," 987.

29. See also ibid., 986.

30. Charlene Allen and Beth Leventhal, "History, Culture, and Identity: What Makes GLBT Battering Different," in *Same-Sex Domestic Violence: Strategies for Change*, ed. Beth Leventhal and Sandra E. Lundy (Thousand Oaks, Calif.: Sage, 1999), 74.

31. Ibid., 73–81.

32. See, for example, *Sorichetti v. City of New York*, 482 N.E. 2d 70 (N.Y. 1985).

33. John Braithwaite, "Youth Development Circles," *Oxford Review of Education* 27 (2001): 241–45.

34. Donna K. Coker, "Enhancing Autonomy for Battered Women: Lessons from Navajo Peacemaking," *UCLA Law Review* 47 (1999): 79.

35. Ibid., 41, 77.

36. Braithwaite, "Restorative Justice," 25.

37. Ibid., 25–26.

38. Coker, "Enhancing Autonomy for Battered Women," 77, 86–87.

39. Braithwaite discusses the unsuccessful nature of conferences that do not allow for a full discussion of the issues in the participants' lives. John Braithwaite, "Restorative Justice and a New Criminal Law of Substance Abuse," *Youth and Society* 33 (2001): 238–40.

40. See Debra Kaminer, Dan J. Stein, Irene Mbanga, Nompumelelo Zungu-Dirwayi, "Forgiveness: Toward an Integration of Theoretical Models," *Psychiatry* 63 (2000): 354, noting that there is evidence that "forgiveness can result in psychological healing and improved mental health" and that "[h]olding the offender accountable through some form of retributive or restorative justice, however, does not negate the possibility of forgiveness."

41. See Dan J. Stein, "Psychiatric Aspects of the Truth and Reconciliation Commission in South Africa," *British Journal of Psychiatry* 173 (1998): 455.

42. Braithwaite, "Restorative Justice," 31.

43. Lawrence W. Sherman, Janell D. Schmidt, Dennis P. Rogan, Douglas A. Smith, Patrick R. Gartin, Ellen G. Cohn, Dean J. Collins, and Anthony R. Bacich, "The Variable Effects of Arrest on Criminal Careers: The Milwaukee Domestic Violence Experiment," *Journal of Criminal Law and Criminology* 83(1992): 137–69.

44. See Kaminer et al., "Forgiveness," 351.

45. Ibid., 350.

46. Virginia Goldner, "The Treatment of Violence and Victimization in Intimate Relationships," *Family Process* 37 (1998): 275–78.

CHAPTER SEVEN
Learning to Listen to Narratives of Intimate Abuse

1. Susan J. Brison, "Violence and the Remaking of a Self," *Chronicle of Higher Education*, January 18, 2002, B10.

2. John P. Wilson, *Trauma, Transformation, and Healing: An Integrative Approach to Theory, Research, and Post-Traumatic Therapy* (New York: Brunner/Mazel, 1989), 212–16.

3. Dutton reports that increased levels of anger in men were correlated with histories of verbal and physical abuse, specifically by their mothers. Donald G. Dutton, *The Domestic Assault of Women: Psychological and Criminal Justice Perspectives* (Vancouver: University of British Columbia Press, 1995), 66.

4. This work is drawn from Gerald Monk, John Winslade, Kathie Crocket, and David Epston, eds., *Narrative Therapy in Practice: The Archaeology of Hope* (San Francisco: Jossey Bass, 1997).

5. Ibid., 85–86.

6. Ibid., 95–98.

7. Ibid., 95.

8. Ibid., 98–116.

9. Virginia Goldner, "The Treatment of Violence and Victimization in Intimate Relationships," *Family Process* 37 (1998): 263–66.

10. See, for example, Elizabeth Schneider, *Battered Women and Feminist Lawmaking* (New Haven, Conn.: Yale University Press, 2000).

11. Janet A. Geller, "Conjoint Therapy for the Treatment of Partner Abuse: Indications and Contradictions," in *Battered Women and Their Families: Intervention Strategies and Treatment Programs*, ed. Albert R. Roberts, 2d ed. (New York: Springer, 1998), 77.

12. Raymond Paternoster, Robert Brame, Ronet Bachman, and Lawrence W. Sherman, "Do Fair Procedures Matter? The Effect of Procedural Justice on Spouse Assault," *Law and Society Review* 31 (1997): 163.

13. These feelings are not uncommon among professionals, especially prosecutors. See, for example, Teri L. Jackson, "Lessons Learned from a Domestic Violence Prosecutor," in *Domestic Violence Law: A Comprehensive Overview of Cases and Sources*, ed. Nancy K. D. Lemon (San Francisco: Austin and Winfield, 1996), 561–62.

14. Cheryl Hanna, "No Right to Choose: Mandated Victim Participation in Domestic Violence Prosecutions," *Harvard Law Review* 109 (1996): 1870.

CHAPTER EIGHT
A Better Way

1. David Goodman, "Why Killers Should Go Free: Lessons from South Africa," *Washington Quarterly* 22 (1999): 172.

2. See Martha Minow, *Between Vengeance and Forgiveness: Facing History after Genocide and Mass Violence* (Boston: Beacon Press, 1998), 52–90.

3. John Braithwaite, "Restorative Justice: Assessing Optimistic and Pessimistic Accounts," *Crime and Justice* 25 (1999): 1.

4. Ibid., 6.

5. Ibid., quoting Tony Marshall.

6. Goodman, "Why Killers Should Go Free," 173.

7. John Braithwaite, "Youth Development Circles," *Oxford Review of Education* 27 (2001): 240–41.

8. Betsy Tsai, note, "The Trend toward Specialized Domestic Violence Courts: Improvements on an Effective Innovation," *Fordham Law Review* 68 (2000): 1321.

9. See, for example, Julie Stubbs, "Domestic Violence and Women's Safety: Feminist Challenges to Restorative Justice," in *Restorative Justice and Family Violence*, ed. Heather Strang and John Braithwaite (Cambridge: Cambridge University Press, 2002), 42–61.

10. Joan Pennell and Gale Burford, "Feminist Praxis: Making Family Group Conferencing Work," in *Restorative Justice and Family Violence*, ed. Heather Strang and John Braithwaite (Cambridge: Cambridge University Press, 2002), 108–27.

11. Braithwaite, "Restorative Justice," 35–38.

12. The Truth and Reconciliation Commission, unlike some other truth commissions, was created by a legislative act following extensive public debate and involvement; Minow, *Between Vengeance and Forgiveness*, 53.

13. Lawrence W. Sherman, Janell D. Schmidt, Dennis P. Rogan, Douglas A. Smith, Patrick R. Gartin, Ellen G. Cohn, Dean J. Collins, and Anthony R. Bacich, "The Variable Effects of Arrest on Criminal Careers: The Milwaukee Domestic Violence Experiment," *Journal of Criminal Law and Criminology* 83 (1992): 137–69.

14. Braithwaite, "Youth Development Circles," 241.

15. See, for example, the specialized domestic violence court described in Randal B. Fritzler and Lenore M. J. Simon, "The Development of a Specialized Domestic Violence Court in Vancouver, Washington, Utilizing Innovative Judicial Paradigms," *University of Missouri at Kansas City Law Review* 69 (2000): 147–48.

16. See articles contained in *Same-Sex Domestic Violence: Strategies for Change*, ed. Beth Leventhal and Sandra E. Lundy (Thousand Oaks, Calif.: Sage, 1999).

17. As domestic abuse treatment provider Tod Augusta-Scott has argued, more than just power and control must be addressed in clinical responses to violence. Tod Augusta-Scott, "Dichotomies in the Power and Control Story: Exploring Multiple Stories about Men Who Choose Abuse in Intimate Relationships," *Gecko: A Journal of Deconstruction and Narrative Ideas in Therapeutic Practice* (2001): 31–68.

18. Fritzler and Simon, "The Development of a Specialized Domestic Violence Court," 167.

19. Tsai points out the inability of "experts" to predict the lethality of abusers. Tsai, "The Trend toward Specialized Domestic Violence Courts," 1293.

20. One such program has convicted offenders wear electronic bracelets set to go off if the offenders are within one hundred feet of a victim's home. See David M. Herszenhorn, "Alarm Helps to Fight Domestic Violence," *New York Times*, July 27, 1999, B3.

21. Sally L. Satel, "It's Always His Fault," *Women's Quarterly*, Independent Women's Forum, Summer 1997, at http://www.iwf.org/pubs/twq/su97a.shtml.

22. Deborah Sontag, "Fierce Entanglements," *New York Times Magazine*, November 17, 2002, 56.

23. Edward W. Gondolf, "Service Barriers for Battered Women with Male Partners in Batterer Programs," *Journal of Interpersonal Violence* 17 (2002): 221.

24. See "UCLA Survey Estimates 11 Million Adult Californians Personally Know Victim of Domestic Violence," press release, Los Angeles, February 19, 2003.

25. Braithwaite, "Restorative Justice," 30–38.

26. Burford and Pennell's work is reported in Braithwaite, "Youth Development Circles," 242.

27. Burford and Pennell's work is reported in Braithwaite, "Restorative Justice," 36.

28. James Ptacek, *Battered Women in the Courtroom: The Power of Judicial Responses* (Boston: Northeastern University Press, 1999).

29. Braithwaite, "Restorative Justice," 56–65.

30. Ibid., 65–67.

31. Ibid., 67–69.

32. Ibid., 70–72.

33. Ibid., 81–82.

34. Ibid.

35. Goodman, "Why Killers Should Go Free," 174.

36. Braithwaite, "Restorative Justice," 82–84.

37. Ibid., 83–84.

38. My previous work on this argument is found in Linda G. Mills, "Killing Her Softly: Intimate Abuse and the Violence of State Intervention," *Harvard Law Review* 113 (1999): 550–613.

39. Andy Geller, George King, Kiran Randhawa, and Stefan C. Friedman, "Two Thoughts on Twin Towers: Poll Reveals Great Divide on Rebuild," *New York Post*, July 14, 2002, 5.

40. See the drawing by Nancy Rubins in Calvin Tomkins, "After the Towers," *New Yorker*, July 15, 2002, 60.

Index

abandonment anxiety, 96

abortion study, 14

abused women: answering the why women stay question on, 60–63; assumption regarding state responsibility to protect, 47; history of law enforcement treatment of, 7–8; law-and-order approach treatment of, 3–4, 5–6; learned helplessness and trauma theory on, 57–60, 90, 91; mainstream feminist advocacy assumptions on, 6–7; ongoing abuse symptoms during ER visits by, 45; physician failure to diagnose symptoms of, 45–46; role in dynamic of intimate abuse by, 8–10, 96–98, 99–100; self-blame by, 99–100; society's collective responsibility to share pain of, 47–48; study on satisfaction with police response by, 42–43; suggested reform policy for arrest "victim-directed" by, 40; suicide attempts/drug and alcohol addiction by, 45; "traumatic bonding" between perpetrators and, 59–60. *See also* women; women in abusive relationships

abusive relationships: answering question of why women stay in, 60–63; challenging thought on reasons women stay in, 30–31; findings on husband/wife violence in, 70; mainstream feminism on reasons that women stay in, 9–10, 27, 57–60; separation of emotional/physical abuse in, 76–79; understanding emotional costs of leaving, 61–62; unique considerations of women in minority religious/racial communities in leaving, 61–62.

See also abused women; dynamic of intimate abuse; women in abusive relationships

African Americans. *See* racial differences

aggression: attachment styles and predisposition to, 92–94; definition and categories of, 69; effect of family on female, 72; implications of couple patterns of, 73–75; learning to be, 90; letting women take responsibility for their, 96–98, 99–100; mainstream feminism dismissal of women's, 3, 6–7, 9, 11–12, 73, 75–76, 95; New Zealand studies on, 69–70; pervasiveness of violence and, 82–84; as powerful female weapon, 76; studies on indirect, 71–72; studies on psychological abuse predicting physical, 73–74; study findings on men's attitudes about women's, 76; study outcomes on physical assault vs., 70; study outcomes on same–sex relationships and, 70–71. *See also* lesbian relationships; LGBT relationships; violence; women's violence

alcohol/drug addiction, 45

American Medical Association, 44

anger: projection of, 2; verbal/physical abuse history and levels of, 167n.3

Aris, Brenda: arrest/conviction of, 67; attachment style of, 94; evidence of projection in judgment of, 81; first meeting with, 67, 146; interaction experiment with, 146–47; law school panel participation by, 147; lessons from case of, 12, 67, 81, 90–92, 94; self-perception as murderer by, 90

deconstruction process, 122–23
denial: of awareness of violence, 2; of September 11th attack by parents, 20–22
Department of Obstetrics and Gynecology (Maricopa Medical Center), 46
dismissing attachment, 92, 93
domestic violence: constructed as gender issue, 8, 10; cycle of violence in, 58; history of approaches to, 7–8; ideological foundation of policies on, 3, 6–7, 9–10, 24, 27–28; mainstream feminist approach to, 3–4, 5–6, 27–32; social construction, 77, 78; social intolerance for, 7; study on failures of incarceration to reduce, 6, 36–46. *See also* intimate abuse; violence
Domestic Violence Unit for the District of Columbia, 48
drug/alcohol addiction, 45
dual arrest problem, 68
Dutton, Donald, 59, 73, 88, 89, 96
dynamic of intimate abuse: addressing role of women in, 8–10, 94–97, 99–100; arguments for development of state insight into, 26–27; attachment styles and, 92–94, 96; description of violent, 94–97; gender differences in reports on violence and, 95–96; implications of psychological-physical aggression patterns in, 73–75; recognizing and understanding, 9–10, 12, 14–15, 30–31; reconceptualizing, 97–100. *See also* abusive relationships; intimate abuse
dynamics of control: determining extent of woman under partner's control, 109–110; differences in LGTB and heterosexual relationships, 110; examining policies undermining sense of control, 11, 47–49; intimate homicides and, 108
Dziuba-Leatherman, Jennifer, 83, 88

Eisikovits, Zvi, 95
Ellard, John H., 66
Ellickson, Phyllis, 72
emotional abuse: correlations of anger levels of men and history of, 167n.3; length of relationship and level of, 109; by mothers on children, 73, 89; as powerful female weapon, 76–77; separation of physical abuse from, 76–79; studies on childhood, 83; studies on indirect aggression and, 71–72; study findings on physical aggression

predicted by, 73–74. *See also* aggression; physical abuse; verbal abuse
empowerment: evidence of therapeutic approaches as leading to, 136; IAC (Intimate Abuse Assessment Team) giving sense of, 141; increased by participation in court remedies, 41–43, 114; mandatory policies as overriding women's, 50–51
equal protection clause (Fourteenth Amendment), 37

Fagan, Ronald W., 45
family violence conferencing approaches, 140
fearful attachment, 92, 93, 94
Finkelhor, David, 83, 88
Flitcraft, Anne, 45
Ford, David A., 41–42
forgiveness: acknowledging responsibility leading to, 113–15; South African Truth and Reconciliation Commission focus on, 134, 135, 141; therapy leading to, 51
Foucault, Michel, 64, 142
Fourteenth Amendment's equal protection clause, 37
freedom to choose, 5
Frontera Prison, 67, 146

gay relationships: dynamics of control in, 110; mainstream feminist thought ignoring violence in, 29–30. *See also* lesbian relationships; LGBT relationships
Gelles, Richard, 70, 88
Gentlewarrier, Sabrina, 71
Gilligan, James, 89, 108
Gondolf, Edward, 139
"good-risk" perpetrators: arrest as deterrent to, 6, 39; defining, 39
Goodrich, Peter. *See* love.
Goodyear-Smith, Felicity A., 76
Gwinn, Casey, 47

Hamberger, L. Kevin, 74
helping professionals: child welfare workers, 80–81; learning to practice IAC narrative therapy, 125–31; projection and judgment by, 2, 79–82; self-reflection work by, 126–127, 131–33. *See also* IAC (Intimate Abuse Circle); child welfare workers; physicians; police; prosecutors; therapists
Hendy, Galla, 101–3, 109–10, 115–18